Fortress
of the Muslim

Invocations from the Qur'ân and Sunnah

Compiled by
Sa'îd bin Wahf Al-Qahtâni

DARUSSALAM
GLOBAL LEADER IN ISLAMIC BOOKS

7th Edition: July 2009

© **Maktaba Dar-us-Salam, 2008**

King Fahd National Library Catalog-in-Publication Data

Maktaba Dar-us-Salam

Fortress of the Muslim, Riyadh

244p, 8x12 cm **ISBN: 978-603-500-021-5**

1-Invocation and award   II-Title

212.93 dc   1429/3673

Legal Deposit no.1429/3673

ISBN: 978-603-500-021-5

CONTENTS

9

11

INTRODUCTION

Surely all praise is for Allāh. We praise Him and seek His help. We seek His forgiveness and we seek refuge in Him from the evil of our own souls and from the wickedness of our deeds. Whomever He guides shall never go astray, and whomever He allows to stray shall never find guidance. I bear witness that none has the right to be worshipped but Allāh, alone, Who has no partner, and I bear witness that Muhammad is His slave and His Messenger. May the peace and blessings of Allāh be upon him and upon his family and his Companions and upon those who follow them in piety until the Day of Judgment.

This book[1] is an abridgment of my earlier work entitled, *Ath-Thikr wad-Du'a wal-'Ilāj bir-Ruqā minal-Kitāb was-Sunnah.*

---

[1] *Hisnul-Muslim min 'Athkāril-Kitāb was-Sunnah,* seventeenth edition printed in the month of Thul-Qa'dah,1416H.

In order to make it small and easily portable, I have chosen only the section on words of remembrance for this abridgment. To achieve this, I only mentioned the text of the words of remembrance instead of the entire *Hadith*. I also limited myself to mentioning only one or two references from the original book for each *Hadith*. Whoever would like to know about the Companion who related a particular *Hadith,* or more information about where it is recorded, should refer to the original work (mentioned above).

I ask Allāh the Glorious, the Mighty, by His beautiful Names and by His sublime Attributes to accept this as having been done sincerely for His sake alone. I ask Him to bring me its benefits during my lifetime and after my death. May those who read it, those who print it, or have had any role in distributing it, benefit from it also. Surely He, the Glorified, is Capable of all things. May the peace and blessings of Allāh be upon our Prophet, Muhammad, and upon his family and Companions and whoever follows them in piety until the Day of Judgment.

Sa'id bin Ali bin Wahaf Al-Qahtāni
Safar,1409H

THE VIRTUE OF REMEMBERING ALLAH

Allāh the All-Mighty has said:

﴿ فَٱذۡكُرُونِىٓ أَذۡكُرۡكُمۡ وَٱشۡكُرُواْ لِى وَلَا تَكۡفُرُونِ ﴾

"Therefore remember Me. I will remember you. Be grateful to Me and never show Me ingratitude."[1]

And He said:

﴿ يَٰٓأَيُّهَا ٱلَّذِينَ ءَامَنُواْ ٱذۡكُرُواْ ٱللَّهَ ذِكۡرًا كَثِيرًا ﴾

"O you who believe, remember Allāh with much remembrance."[2]

And He said:

﴿ وَٱلذَّٰكِرِينَ ٱللَّهَ كَثِيرًا وَٱلذَّٰكِرَٰتِ أَعَدَّ ٱللَّهُ لَهُم مَّغۡفِرَةً وَأَجۡرًا عَظِيمًا ﴾

---

[1] Al-Baqarah 2:152. Meanings of 'Āyāt from the Qur'ān in this book are based on The Interpretation of the Meanings of the Noble Qur'ān, by Dr. Muhammad Muhsin Khan, Darussalam, Riyadh, 1994.
[2] Al-Ahzāb 33:41.

"And the men and women who remember Allāh frequently, Allāh has prepared for them forgiveness and a great reward."[1]

And He said:

﴿وَٱذْكُر رَّبَّكَ فِي نَفْسِكَ تَضَرُّعًا وَخِيفَةً وَدُونَ ٱلْجَهْرِ مِنَ ٱلْقَوْلِ بِٱلْغُدُوِّ وَٱلْآصَالِ وَلَا تَكُن مِّنَ ٱلْغَٰفِلِينَ﴾

"And remember your Lord by your tongue and within yourself, humbly and in awe, without loudness, by words in the morning and in the afternoon, and be not among those who are neglectful."[2]

The Prophet ﷺ said: "He who remembers his Lord and he who does not remember his Lord, are like the living and the dead."[3]

---

[1] Al-Aḥzāb 33:35.

[2] Al-A'rāf 7:205.

[3] Al-Bukhāri, cf., Al-Asqalāni, Fatḥul-Bāri 11/208; Muslim 1/539 with the wording: "The house in which Allāh is remembered and the

17

And he said, "Shall I not inform you all of the best of your works, the purest of them with your Master (Allāh), the loftiest of them in your stations, the thing that is better for you than spending gold and silver (in charity), and better for you than meeting your enemies and slaying them and being slain by them?" They (the Companions) said, "Of course!" He said, "Remembrance of Allāh, the Most High."[1]

And he said: "Allāh the Most High says, 'I am with my slave when he thinks of Me and I am with him when he mentions Me. For if he mentions Me to himself, I mention him to Myself; and if he mentions Me in a gathering, I mention him in a superior gathering. If he approaches Me by a hand's width, I

---

house in which Allāh is not remembered are like the living and the dead."

[1] At-Tirmithi 5/459, Ibn Mājah 2/1245. See Al-Albāni, Sahih Ibn Mājah 2/316 and Sahih At-Tirmithi 3/139.

approach him by an arm's length; and if he approaches me by an arm's length, I approach him by two arms' length. And if he comes to Me walking, I hasten to him swiftly.' "[1]

Abdullah bin Busr ☼ said that a man asked the Prophet ﷺ, "O Messenger of Allāh! Verily, the sanctions of Islam have become too numerous for me (to perform them all). Inform me of something (simple) that I may always adhere to." The Prophet ﷺ said, "Let your tongue always be moist with the remembrance of Allāh."[2]

And he said: "Whoever reads one letter from the Book of Allāh, will receive one *Hasanah* (reward for a good deed), and one *Hasanah* comes with ten like it. I do not say that *Alif-Lām-Mīm* is a letter.

---

[1] Al-Bukhāri 8/171, Muslim 4/2061; this wording is from Al-Bukhāri.

[2] At-Tirmithi 5/458, Ibn Mājah 2/1246. See Al-Albāni, *Sahih At-Tirmithi* 3/139 and *Sahih Ibn Mājah* 2/317.

Indeed *Alif* is a letter, and *Lām* is a letter, and *Mīm* is a letter."[1]

'Uqbah bin 'Amir ⬥ said: The Messenger of Allāh ﷺ came out (from his house) and we were on the porch (*As-Suffah*). So he said, "Who of you would like to go out in the morning everyday to the valley of *Buthan* or *Al-'Aqeeq* and come back with two large she-camels without committing any sin or severing the family ties?" We replied, "O Messenger of Allāh! All of us would like this." So he said, "Would one of you not go to the *Masjid* and learn or recite two Verses from the Book of Allāh, the Mighty and Majestic? That would be better for him than two she-camels. And three Verses would be better for him than three she-camels. And four Verses would be better than four she-camels, and whatever their number may be of camels."[2]

And he said: "Whoever sits and does not

---

[1] At-Tirmithī 5/175. See Al-Albāni, *Sahih At-Tirmithī* 3/9 and *Sahihul-Jāmi' As-Saghīr* 5/340.
[2] Muslim 1/553.

mention the Name of Allāh (before he rises), will find it a cause of sorrow from Allāh. Whoever lies down to sleep and does not mention the Name of Allāh before rising, will find it a cause of sorrow from Allāh."[1]

And the Prophet ﷺ said: "No people sit in an assembly without mentioning Allāh, and without asking Allāh for blessings on their Prophet, except that it will be a cause of sorrow upon them. Thus, if He (Allāh) wishes He will punish them, and if He wishes He will forgive them."[2]

And he said: "No people may rise from an assembly in which they have failed to mention the Name of Allāh without it being as if they were getting off a dead donkey's rotting back, and it would be a cause of grief for them."[3]

---

[1] Abu Dawud 4/264. See Al-Albāni, *Sahihul-Jāmi' As-Saghīr* 5/342.

[2] At-Tirmithi. See Al-Albāni, *Sahih At-Tirmithi* 3/140.

[3] Abu Dawud 4/264, Ahmad 2/389. See Al-Albāni, *Sahihul-Jāmi'* 5/176.

1. Supplications for when you wake up

١-«الْحَمْدُ لله الَّذِي أَحْيَانَا بَعْدَ مَا أَمَاتَنَا وَإِلَيْهِ النُّشُورُ»

1. *Alhamdu lillaahil-lathee 'ahyaanaa ba'da maa 'amaatanaa wa'ilayhin-nushoor.*

Praise is to Allāh Who gives us life after He has caused us to die and to Him is the return.[1]

٢-«لَا إِلَهَ إِلَّا اللهُ وَحْدَهُ لَا شَرِيكَ لَهُ، لَهُ الْمُلْكُ وَلَهُ الْحَمْدُ، وَهُوَ عَلَى كُلِّ شَيْءٍ قَدِيرٌ. سُبْحَانَ اللهِ، وَالْحَمْدُ للهِ، وَلَا إِلَهَ إِلَّا اللهُ، وَاللهُ أَكْبَرُ، وَلَا حَوْلَ وَلَا قُوَّةَ إِلَّا بِاللهِ الْعَلِيِّ الْعَظِيمِ، رَبِّ اغْفِرْلِي»

2. *Laa 'ilaaha 'illallaahu wahdahu laa shareeka lahu, lahul-mulku wa lahul-hamdu, wa Huwa 'alaa kulli shay'in Qadeer. Subhaanallaahi,*

---

[1] Al-Bukhāri, cf. Al-Asqalāni, *Fathul-Bāri* 11/113; Muslim 4/2083.

walhamdu lillaahi, wa laa 'ilaaha 'illallaahu,
wallaahu 'akbar, wa laa hawla wa laa
Quwwata 'illaa billaahil-'Aliyyil-'Adheem,
Rabbighfir lee.

There is none worthy of worship but
Allāh alone, Who has no partner. His is
the dominion and to Him belongs all
praise, and He is Able to do all things.
Glory is to Allāh. Praise is to Allāh. There
is none worthy of worship but Allāh.
Allāh is the Most Great. There is no might
and no power except by Allāh's leave, the
Exalted, the Mighty. My Lord, forgive
me.[1]

٣-«الْحَمْدُ لله الَّذِي عَافَانِي فِي جَسَدِي، وَرَدَّ
عَلَيَّ رُوحِي، وَأَذِنَ لِي بِذِكْرِهِ»

---

[1] Whoever says this will be forgiven, and if
he supplicates Allāh, his prayer will be
answered; if he performs ablution and prays,
his prayer will be accepted. *Al-Bukhāri, cf. Al-
Asqalāni, Fathul-Bāri* 3/39, among others. The
wording here is from Ibn Mājah 2/335.

3. Alhamdu lillaahil-lathee 'aafaanee fee jasadee, wa radda 'alayya roohee, wa 'athina lee bithikrihi.

Praise is to Allāh Who gave strength to my body and returned my soul to me and permitted me to remember Him.[1]

٤ - ﴿إِنَّ فِى خَلْقِ ٱلسَّمَٰوَٰتِ وَٱلْأَرْضِ وَٱخْتِلَٰفِ ٱلَّيْلِ وَٱلنَّهَارِ لَءَايَٰتٍ لِّأُو۟لِى ٱلْأَلْبَٰبِ ٠ ٱلَّذِينَ يَذْكُرُونَ ٱللَّهَ قِيَٰمًا وَقُعُودًا وَعَلَىٰ جُنُوبِهِمْ وَيَتَفَكَّرُونَ فِى خَلْقِ ٱلسَّمَٰوَٰتِ وَٱلْأَرْضِ رَبَّنَا مَا خَلَقْتَ هَٰذَا بَٰطِلًا سُبْحَٰنَكَ فَقِنَا عَذَابَ ٱلنَّارِ ٠ رَبَّنَآ إِنَّكَ مَن تُدْخِلِ ٱلنَّارَ فَقَدْ أَخْزَيْتَهُۥ وَمَا لِلظَّٰلِمِينَ مِنْ أَنصَارٍ ٠ رَبَّنَآ إِنَّنَا سَمِعْنَا مُنَادِيًا يُنَادِى لِلْإِيمَٰنِ أَنْ ءَامِنُوا۟ بِرَبِّكُمْ فَـَٔامَنَّا رَبَّنَا فَٱغْفِرْ لَنَا ذُنُوبَنَا وَكَفِّرْ عَنَّا سَيِّـَٔاتِنَا وَتَوَفَّنَا مَعَ ٱلْأَبْرَارِ ٠ رَبَّنَا وَءَاتِنَا مَا وَعَدتَّنَا عَلَىٰ رُسُلِكَ وَلَا تُخْزِنَا يَوْمَ ٱلْقِيَٰمَةِ إِنَّكَ لَا تُخْلِفُ ٱلْمِيعَادَ ٠ فَٱسْتَجَابَ لَهُمْ رَبُّهُمْ أَنِّى لَآ أُضِيعُ عَمَلَ عَٰمِلٍ مِّنكُم مِّن ذَكَرٍ أَوْ أُنثَىٰ بَعْضُكُم

[1] At-Tirmithi 5/473. See Al-Albāni's Sahih At-Tirmithi 3/144.

مِنْ بَعْضٍ فَالَّذِينَ هَاجَرُوا وَأُخْرِجُوا مِنْ دِيَـٰرِهِمْ وَأُوذُوا فِى
سَبِيلِى وَقَـٰتَلُوا وَقُتِلُوا لَأُكَفِّرَنَّ عَنْهُمْ سَيِّئَاتِهِمْ وَلَأُدْخِلَنَّهُمْ
جَنَّـٰتٍ تَجْرِى مِن تَحْتِهَا الْأَنْهَـٰرُ ثَوَابًا مِّنْ عِندِ اللَّهِ وَاللَّهُ
عِندَهُ حُسْنُ الثَّوَابِ ○ لَا يَغُرَّنَّكَ تَقَلُّبُ الَّذِينَ كَفَرُوا فِى
الْبِلَـٰدِ ○ مَتَـٰعٌ قَلِيلٌ ثُمَّ مَأْوَىٰهُمْ جَهَنَّمُ وَبِئْسَ الْمِهَادُ ○
لَـٰكِنِ الَّذِينَ اتَّقَوْا رَبَّهُمْ لَهُمْ جَنَّـٰتٌ تَجْرِى مِن تَحْتِهَا الْأَنْهَـٰرُ
خَـٰلِدِينَ فِيهَا نُزُلًا مِّنْ عِندِ اللَّهِ وَمَا عِندَ اللَّهِ خَيْرٌ لِّلْأَبْرَارِ ○
وَإِنَّ مِنْ أَهْلِ الْكِتَـٰبِ لَمَن يُؤْمِنُ بِاللَّهِ وَمَا أُنزِلَ إِلَيْكُمْ وَمَا
أُنزِلَ إِلَيْهِمْ خَـٰشِعِينَ لِلَّهِ لَا يَشْتَرُونَ بِـَٔايَـٰتِ اللَّهِ ثَمَنًا قَلِيلًا
أُولَـٰئِكَ لَهُمْ أَجْرُهُمْ عِندَ رَبِّهِمْ إِنَّ اللَّهَ سَرِيعُ
الْحِسَابِ ○ يَـٰٓأَيُّهَا الَّذِينَ ءَامَنُوا اصْبِرُوا وَصَابِرُوا
وَرَابِطُوا وَاتَّقُوا اللَّهَ لَعَلَّكُمْ تُفْلِحُونَ ﴾

4. 'Inna fee khalqis-samaawaati wal'ardhi
wakhtilaafil-layli wannahaari la'aayaatil-li
'oolil'albaab. Allatheena yathkuroon-allaaha
qiyaaman wa qu'oodan wa 'alaa junoobihim
wa yatafakkaroona fee khalqis-samaawaati

*wal'ardhi Rabbanaa maa khalaqta haathaa
baatilan subhaanaka faqinaa 'athaaban-naar.
Rabbanaa 'innaka man tudkhilin-naara faqad
'akhzaytahu wa maa lidhdhalimeena min
'ansaar. Rabbanaa 'innanaa sami'naa
munaadiyan yunaadee lil'eemaani 'an
'aaminoo birabbikum fa'aamannaa, Rabbanaa
faghfir lanaa thunoobanaa wa kaffir 'annaa
sayyi'aatinaa wa tawaffanaa ma'al-'abraar.
Rabbanaa wa 'aatinaa maa wa'adtanaa 'alaa
rusulika wa laa tukhzinaa yawmal-qiyaamati,
'innaka laa tukhliful-mee'aad. Fastajaaba
lahum Rabbuhum 'annee laa 'udhee'u 'amala
'aamilim-minkum min thakarin 'aw 'unthaa,
ba'dhukum mim ba'dh, fallatheena haajaroo
wa 'ukhrijoo min diyaarihim wa 'oothoo fee
sabeelee wa qaataloo wa qutiloo la'ukaffiranna
'anhum sayyi'aatihim wa la'udkhilannahum
jannaatin tajree min tahtihal-'anhaaru
thawaaban min 'indillaah, wallaahu 'indahu
husnuth-thawaab. Laa yaghur-rannaka
taqallubul-latheena kafaroo fil-bilaad.
Mataa'un qaleelun thumma ma'waahum
jahannam, wa bi'sal-mihaad. Laakinil-*

latheenat-taqaw Rabbahum lahum jannaatun tajree min tahtihal-'anhaaru khaalideena feehaa nuzulam-min 'indillaah, wa maa 'indallaahi khayrul-lil'abraar. Wa 'inna min 'ahlil-kitaabi laman yu'minu billaahi wa maa 'unzila 'ilaykum wa maa 'unzila 'ilayhim khaashi'eena lillaahi laa yashtaroona bi'aayaatillaahi thamanan qaleela, 'oolaa'ika lahum 'ajruhum 'inda Rabbihim, 'innallaaha saree'ul-hisaab. Yaa'ayyuhal-latheena 'aamanus-biroo wa saabiroo wa raabitoo wattaqul-laaha la'allakum tuflihoon.

Verily! In the creation of the heavens and the earth, and in the alternation of night and day, there are indeed Signs for men of understanding. Those who remember Allāh standing, sitting and lying down on their sides, and think deeply about the creation of the heavens and the earth, (saying:) "Our Lord! You have not created this without purpose, glory is to You! Give us salvation from the torment of the Fire. Our Lord! Verily, whom You admit to the Fire, indeed, You have

27

disgraced him, and never will the oppressors find any helpers. Our Lord! Verily, we have heard the call of one calling to Faith (saying:) 'Believe in your Lord,' and we have believed. Our Lord! Forgive us our sins and expiate from us our evil deeds, and make us die in the state of righteousness together with the pious and righteous slaves. Our Lord! Grant us what You promised us through Your Messengers, and disgrace us not on the Day of Resurrection, for You never break (Your) promise.'' So, their Lord answered them (saying): "Never will I allow to be lost the work of any of you, be he male or female. You issue forth one from another, so those who emigrated and were driven out from their homes, and suffered harm in My Cause and who fought, and were killed in My Cause, verily, I will expiate from them their evil deeds and admit them into Gardens under which rivers flow; a reward from Allāh, and with Allāh is the best of rewards." Let not the free disposal of the disbelievers through out the land deceive you. A brief enjoyment; then, their ultimate abode is Hell; and worst indeed is that place for rest. But, for those who fear their Lord, are Gardens under which rivers flow; therein are they to dwell forever, and entertainment from Allāh; and that which is with Allāh is the best for the pious and righteous slaves. And there are, certainly, among the people of the Scripture, those who believe in Allāh and in that which has been revealed to you, and in that which has been revealed to them, humbling themselves before Allāh. They do not sell the Verses of Allāh for a little price, for them is a reward with their Lord. Surely, Allāh is Swift in account. O you who believe! Have patience and contend in patience, be vigilant and informed, and fear Allāh, so that you may be successful.[1]

---

[1] Qur'ān Aal-'Imrān 3:190-200; Al-Bukhāri, cf. Al-Asqalāni, Fathul-Bāri 8/237; Muslim 1/530.

2. Invocation when getting dressed

٥-«الْحَمْدُ لله الَّذِي كَسَانِي هَذَا (الثَّوبَ)
وَرَزَقَنِيهِ مِنْ غَيْرِ حَوْلٍ مِنِّي وَلَا قُوَّةٍ..».

5. *Alhamdu lillaahil-lathee kasaanee haathaa (aththawba) wa razaqaneehi min ghayri hawlim-minnee wa laa quwwatin.*

Praise is to Allāh Who has clothed me with this (garment) and provided it for me, though I was powerless myself and incapable.[1]

3. Invocation when putting on new clothes

٦-«اللَّهُمَّ لَكَ الْحَمْدُ أَنْتَ كَسَوْتَنِيهِ، أَسْأَلُكَ
مِنْ خَيْرِهِ وَخَيْرِ مَا صُنِعَ لَهُ، وَأَعُوذُ بِكَ مِنْ
شَرِّهِ وَشَرِّ مَا صُنِعَ لَهُ».

6. *Allaahumma lakal-hamdu 'Anta kasawtaneehi, 'as'aluka min khayrihi wa*

---

[1] Al-Bukhārī, Muslim, Abu Dawud, Ibn Mājah, At-Tirmithī. See also *'Irwa'ul-Ghalīl* 7/47.

khayri maa suni'a lahu, wa 'a'oothu bika min sharrihi wa sharri ma suni'a lahu.

O Allāh, praise is to You. You have clothed me. I ask You for its goodness and the goodness of what it has been made for, and I seek Your protection from the evil of it and the evil of what it has been made for.[1]

4. Invocations for someone who has put on new clothes

٧-«تُبْلِي وَيُخْلِفُ اللهُ تَعَالَى».

7. *Tublee wa yukhliful-laahu ta'aalaa.*

May Allāh replace it when it is worn out.[2]

٨-«الْبَسْ جَدِيدًا، وَعِشْ حَمِيدًا، وَمُتْ شَهِيدًا».

8. *Ilbas jadeedan, wa 'ish hameedan, wa mut shaheedan.*

---

[1] Abu Dawud and At-Tirmithi. See also Al-Albāni, *Mukhtasar Shamā'il At-Tirmithi*, p. 47.

[2] Abu Dawud 4/41. See also Al-Albāni *Sahih Abu Dawud* 2/760.

Put on new clothes, live a praise-worthy life and die as a martyr.[1]

5. What to say when undressing

٩- «بِسْمِ اللهِ».

9. *Bismillaahi.*

In the Name of Allāh.[2]

6. Invocation for entering the restroom

١٠- «[بِسْمِ اللهِ] اللَّهُمَّ إِنِّي أَعُوذُ بِكَ مِنَ الْخُبْثِ وَالْخَبَائِثِ».

10. *[Bismillaahi] Allaahumma 'innee 'a'oothu bika minal-khubthi walkhabaa'ith.*

(Before entering) [In the Name of Allāh]. (Then) O Allāh, I seek protection in You from the male and female unclean spirits.[3]

---

[1] Ibn Mājah 2/1178, Al-Baghawi 12/41. See also Al-Albāni, *Sahih Ibn Mājah* 2/275.

[2] At-Tirmithi 2/505, among others. See *'Irwa'ul-Ghalīl* no. 49 and *Sahihul-Jāmi'* 3/203.

[3] Al-Bukhāri 1/45, Muslim 1/283. The addition of *Bismillāh* at its beginning was

7. Invocation for leaving the restroom

١١ - «غُفْرَانَكَ» .

11. *Ghufraanaka.*

I seek Your forgiveness.[1]

8. What to say before performing ablution

١٢ - «بِسْمِ اللهِ» .

12. *Bismillaahi.*

In the Name of Allāh.[2]

9. What to say upon completing ablution

١٣ - «أَشْهَدُ أَنْ لَا إِلَهَ إِلَّا اللهُ وَحْدَهُ لَا شَرِيكَ

---

reported by Saʿīd bin Mansûr. See *Fathul-Bāri*
1/244.

[1] Abu Dawud, Ibn Mājah and At-Tirmithi.
An-Nasāʾi recorded it in *ʿAmalul-Yawm wal-Laylah*. Also see the checking of Ibn Al-Qayyim's *Zādul-Maʿād*, 2/387.

[2] Abu Dawud, Ibn Mājah, and Ahmad. See
also Al-Albāni, *ʾIrwaʾul-Ghalīl* 1/122.

لَهُ، وَأَشْهَدُ أَنَّ مُحَمَّدًا عَبْدُهُ وَرَسُولُهُ. . .».

13. 'Ash-hadu 'an laa 'ilaaha 'illallaahu wahdahu laa shareeka lahu wa 'ash-hadu 'anna Muhammadan 'abduhu wa Rasooluhu.

I bear witness that none has the right to be worshipped but Allāh alone, Who has no partner; and I bear witness that Muhammad is His slave and His Messenger.[1]

١٤-«اللَّهُمَّ اجْعَلْنِي مِنَ التَّوَّابِينَ وَاجْعَلْنِي مِنَ الْمُتَطَهِّرِينَ».

14. Allaahummaj'alnee minat-tawwaabeena waj'alnee minal-mutatahhireen.

O Allāh, make me among those who turn to You in repentance, and make me among those who are purified.[2]

١٥-«سُبْحَانَكَ اللَّهُمَّ وَبِحَمْدِكَ، أَشْهَدُ أَنْ لَا

---

[1] Muslim 1/209.
[2] At-Tirmithi 1/78. See also Al-Albāni, Sahih At-Tirmithi 1/18.

إِلَهَ إِلَّا أَنْتَ، أَسْتَغْفِرُكَ وَأَتُوبُ إِلَيْكَ».

15. *Subhaanaka Allaahumma wa bihamdika,
'ash-hadu 'an laa 'ilaaha 'illaa 'Anta,
'astaghfiruka wa 'atoobu 'ilayk.*

Glory is to You, O Allāh, and praise; I
bear witness that there is none worthy of
worship but You. I seek Your forgiveness
and turn to You in repentance.[1]

10. What to say when leaving the home

١٦ـ «بِسْمِ اللهِ، تَوَكَّلْتُ عَلَى اللهِ، وَلَا حَوْلَ
وَلَا قُوَّةَ إِلَّا بِاللهِ».

16. *Bismillaahi, tawakkaltu 'alallaahi, wa laa
hawla wa laa quwwata 'illaa billaah.*

In the Name of Allāh, I have placed my
trust in Allāh, there is no might and no
power except by Allāh.[2]

---

[1] An-Nasā'i, *'Amalul-Yawm wal-Laylah*, p. 173.
See also Al-Albāni, *'Irwa'ul-Ghalil* 1/135 and 2/94.
[2] Abu Dawud 4/325, At-Tirmithi 5/490. See
also Al-Albāni, *Sahih At-Tirmithi* 3/151.

١٧-«اللَّهُمَّ إِنِّي أَعُوذُ بِكَ أَنْ أَضِلَّ، أَوْ أُضَلَّ، أَوْ أَزِلَّ، أَوْ أُزَلَّ، أَوْ أَظْلِمَ، أَوْ أُظْلَمَ، أَوْ أَجْهَلَ، أَوْ يُجْهَلَ عَلَيَّ».

17. *Allaahumma 'innee 'a'oothu bika 'an 'adhilla, 'aw 'udhalla, 'aw 'azilla, 'aw 'uzalla, 'aw 'adhlima, 'aw 'udhlama, 'aw 'ajhala 'aw yujhala 'alayya.*

O Allāh, I seek refuge in You lest I misguide others, or I am misguided by others, lest I cause others to err or I am caused to err, lest I abuse others or be abused, and lest I behave foolishly or meet with the foolishness of others.[1]

11. What to say when entering the home

١٨-«بِسْمِ اللهِ وَلَجْنَا، وَبِسْمِ اللهِ خَرَجْنَا، وَعَلَى اللهِ رَبِّنَا تَوَكَّلْنَا».

---

[1] Abu Dawud, Ibn Mājah, An-Nasā'i, At-Tirmithi. See also Al-Albāni, *Sahih At-Tirmithi* 3/152 and *Sahih Ibn Mājah* 2/336.

18. *Bismillaahi walajnaa, wa bismillaahi kharajnaa, wa 'alallaahi Rabbinaa tawakkalnaa.*

In the Name of Allāh we enter, in the Name of Allāh we leave, and upon Allāh our Lord we depend [then say *As-Salaamu 'Alaykum* to those present].[1]

12. Invocation for going to the mosque

١٩ –«اللَّهُمَّ اجْعَلْ فِي قَلْبِي نُورًا، وَفِي لِسَانِي نُورًا، وَفِي سَمْعِي نُورًا، وَفِي بَصَرِي نُورًا، وَمِنْ فَوْقِي نُورًا، وَمِنْ تَحْتِي نُورًا، وَعَنْ يَمِينِي نُورًا، وَعَنْ شِمَالِي نُورًا، وَمِنْ أَمَامِي نُورًا، وَمِنْ خَلْفِي نُورًا، وَاجْعَلْ فِي نَفْسِي نُورًا، وَأَعْظِمْ لِي نُورًا، وَعَظِّمْ لِي نُورًا، وَاجْعَلْ لِي نُورًا، وَاجْعَلْنِي نُورًا، اللَّهُمَّ أَعْطِنِي نُورًا، وَاجْعَلْ فِي

---

[1] Abu Dawud 4/325. Muslim (*Hadith* no. 2018) says that one should mention the Name of Allāh when entering the home and when beginning to eat; and that the devil, hearing this, says: "There is no shelter for us here tonight and no food."

عَصَبِي نُورًا، وَفِي لَحْمِي نُورًا، وَفِي دَمِي نُورًا، وَفِي شَعْرِي نُورًا، وَفِي بَشَرِي نُورًا،، «اللَّهُمَّ اجْعَلْ لِي نُورًا فِي قَبْرِي .. وَنُورًا فِي عِظَامِي» [«وَزِدْنِي نُورًا، وَزِدْنِي نُورًا، وَزِدْنِي نُورًا»] [«وَهَبْ لِي نُورًا عَلَى نُورٍ»].

19. Allaahummaj'al fee qalbee nooran, wa fee lisaanee nooran, wa fee sam'ee nooran, wa fee basaree nooran, wa min fawqee nooran, wa min tahtee nooran, wa 'an yameenee nooran, wa 'an shimaalee nooran, wa min 'amaamee nooran, wa min khalfee nooran, waj'al fee nafsee nooran, wa 'a'dhim lee nooran, wa 'adhdhim lee nooran, waj'al lee nooran, waj'alnee nooran, Allaahumma 'a'tinee nooran, waj'al fee 'asabee nooran, wa fee lahmee nooran, wa fee damee nooran, wa fee sha'ree nooran, wa fee basharee nooran. [Allaahummaj'al lee nooran fee qabree wa nooran fee 'idhaamee.] [Wa zidnee nooran, wa zidnee nooran, wa zidnee nooran.] [Wa hab lee nooran 'alaa noor.]

O Allāh, place light in my heart, and on my tongue light, and in my ears light and in my sight light, and above me light, and below me light, and to my right light, and to my left light, and before me light and behind me light. Place in my soul light. Magnify for me light, and amplify for me light. Make for me light and make me a light. O Allāh, grant me light, and place light in my nerves, and in my body light and in my blood light and in my hair light and in my skin light.[1] [O Allāh, make for me a light in my grave... and a light in my bones.][2] [Increase me in light, increase me in light, increase me in light.][3] [Grant me light upon light.][4]

---

[1] Up to this point was reported by Al-Bukhāri 11/116 (*Hadith* no. 6316) and by Muslim 1/526, 529-530 (*Hadith* no. 763).

[2] At-Tirmithi 5/483 (*Hadith* no. 3419).

[3] Al-Bukhāri in *Al-'Adab Al-Mufrad* (*Hadith* no. 695), p. 258. See also Al-Albāni, *Sahih Al-'Adab Al-Mufrad* (no. 536).

[4] Al-Bukhāri, cf. Al-Asqalāni, *Fathul-Bāri* 11/118.

13. Invocation for entering the mosque

٢٠-«أَعُوذُ بِاللهِ الْعَظِيمِ، وَبِوَجْهِهِ الْكَرِيمِ،
وَسُلْطَانِهِ الْقَدِيمِ، مِنَ الشَّيْطَانِ الرَّجِيمِ». [بِسْمِ
اللهِ، وَالصَّلَاةُ] [وَالسَّلَامُ عَلَى رَسُولِ اللهِ]
«اللَّهُمَّ افْتَحْ لِي أَبْوَابَ رَحْمَتِكَ».

20. 'A'oothu billaahil-'Adheem, wa bi-Wajhihil-Kareem, wa Sultaanihil-qadeem, minash-Shaytaanir-rajeem. [Bismillaahi, wassalaatu.] [Wassalaamu 'alaa Rasoolillaahi.] Allaahum-maftah lee 'abwaaba rahmatika.

I seek refuge in Almighty Allāh, by His Noble Face, by His primordial power, from Satan the outcast.[1] [In the Name of Allāh, and blessings.][2] [And peace be upon the Messenger of Allāh.][3] O Allāh,

---

[1] Abu Dawud and Al-Albāni, *Sahihul-Jāmi' As-Saghir* (*Hadith* no. 4591).

[2] Ibn As-Sunni (*Hadith* no. 88), graded good by Al-Albāni.

[3] Abu Dawud 1/126, see also Al-Albāni, *Sahihul-Jāmi' As-Saghīr* 1/528.

open before me the doors of Your mercy.[1]

14. Invocation for leaving the mosque

٢١-«بِسْمِ اللهِ وَالصَّلَاةُ وَالسَّلَامُ عَلَى رَسُولِ اللهِ، اللَّهُمَّ إِنِّي أَسْأَلُكَ مِنْ فَضْلِكَ، اللَّهُمَّ اعْصِمْنِي مِنَ الشَّيْطَانِ الرَّجِيمِ».

21. Bismillaahi wassalaatu wassalaamu 'alaa Rasoolillaahi, Allaahumma 'innee 'as'aluka min fadhlika, Allaahumma'simnee minash-Shaytaanir-rajeem.

In the Name of Allāh, and peace and blessings be upon the Messenger of Allāh. O Allāh, I ask for Your favor, O Allāh, protect me from Satan the outcast.[2]

---

[1] Muslim 1/494. There is also a report in Sunan Ibn Mājah on the authority of Fātimah ﷺ : "O Allāh, forgive me my sins and open for me the doors of Your mercy." It was graded authentic by Al-Albāni due to supporting Ahadith. See Sahih Ibn Mājah 1/128-9.

[2] ibid.

15. What to say upon hearing the 'Athān (call to prayer)

22. Repeat what the Mu'aththin says, except for when he says:

«حَيَّ عَلَى الصَّلَاةِ وَحَيَّ عَلَى الْفَلَاحِ» .

Hayya 'alas-Salaah (hasten to the prayer) and Hayya 'alal-Falaah (hasten to salvation). Here you should say:

«لَا حَوْلَ وَلَا قُوَّةَ إِلَّا بِاللهِ» .

Laa hawla wa laa quwwata 'illaa billaah.

There is no might and no power except by Allāh.[1]

٢٣-«وَأَنَا أَشْهَدُ أَنْ لَا إِلَهَ إِلَّا اللهُ وَحْدَهُ لَا
شَرِيكَ لَهُ وَأَنَّ مُحَمَّدًا عَبْدُهُ وَرَسُولُهُ، رَضِيتُ
بِاللهِ رَبًّا وَبِمُحَمَّدٍ رَسُولًا وَبِالْإِسْلَامِ دِينًا» .

23. Wa 'anaa 'ash-hadu 'an laa 'ilaaha 'illallaahu wahdahu laa shareeka lahu wa 'anna Muhammadan 'abduhu wa Rasooluhu,

---

[1] Al-Bukhāri 1/152, Muslim 1/288.

radheetu billaahi Rabban, wa bi- Muhammadin Rasoolan wa bil'islaami deenan.

I bear witness that none has the right to be worshipped but Allāh alone, Who has no partner, and that Muhammad is His slave and His Messenger. I am pleased with Allāh as my Lord, with Muhammad as my Messenger and with Islam as my religion.[1] [To be recited in Arabic after the *Mu'aththin's Tashahhud* or the words of affirmation of Faith].[2]

24. After replying to the call of *Mu'aththin*, you should recite in Arabic Allāh's blessings on the Prophet.[3]

٢٥- «اللّهُمَّ رَبَّ هَذِهِ الدَّعْوَةِ التَّامَّةِ، وَالصَّلَاةِ الْقَائِمَةِ، آتِ مُحَمَّدًا الْوَسِيلَةَ وَالْفَضِيلَةَ، وَابْعَثْهُ مَقَامًا مَحْمُودًا الَّذِي وَعَدْتَهُ، [إِنَّكَ لَا تُخْلِفُ الْمِيعَادَ]»

---

[1] Muslim 1/290.

[2] Ibn Khuzaymah 1/220.

[3] Muslim 1/288.

25. *Allaahumma Rabba haathihid-da'watit-taammati wassalaatil-qaa'imati, 'aati Muhammadanil-waseelata walfadheelata, wab'ath-hu maqaamam-mahmoodanil-lathee wa'adtahu, ['innaka laa tukhliful-mee'aad].*

O Allāh, Lord of this perfect call and established prayer. Grant Muhammad the intercession and favor, and raise him to the honored station You have promised him, [verily You do not neglect promises].[1]

26. Between the call to prayer and the *'Iqāmah*, you should supplicate Allāh for yourself. Invocation during this time is not rejected.[2]

16. Invocations for the beginning of the prayer

٢٧ – «اللَّهُمَّ بَاعِدْ بَيْنِي وَبَيْنَ خَطَايَايَ كَمَا

---

[1] Al-Bukhāri 1/152, and the addition between brackets is from Al-Bayhaqi 1/410 with a good (*Hasan*) chain of narration. See 'Abdul-Azīz bin Bāz's *Tuhfatul-'Akhyār*, pg. 38.
[2] At-Tirmithi, Abu Dawud, Ahmad. See also Al-Albāni, *'Irwā'ul-Ghalil* 1/262.

بَاعَدْتَ بَيْنَ الْمَشْرِقِ وَالْمَغْرِبِ، اللَّهُمَّ نَقِّنِي مِنْ خَطَايَايَ، كَمَا يُنَقَّى الثَّوْبُ الْأَبْيَضُ مِنَ الدَّنَسِ، اللَّهُمَّ اغْسِلْنِي مِنْ خَطَايَايَ بِالثَّلْجِ وَالْمَاءِ وَالْبَرَدِ».

27. *Allaahumma baa'id baynee wa bayna khataayaaya kamaa baa'adta baynal-mashriqi walmaghribi, Allaahumma naqqinee min khataayaaya kamaa yunaqqath-thawbul-'abyadhu minad-danasi, Allaahum-maghsilnee min khataayaaya, bith-thalji walmaa'i walbarad.*

O Allāh, separate me from my sins as You have separated the East from the West. O Allāh, cleanse me of my transgressions as the white garment is cleansed of stains. O Allāh, wash away my sins with ice and water and frost.[1]

٢٨-«سُبْحَانَكَ اللَّهُمَّ وَبِحَمْدِكَ، وَتَبَارَكَ اسْمُكَ، وَتَعَالَى جَدُّكَ، وَلَا إِلَهَ غَيْرُكَ».

---

[1] Al-Bukhāri 1/181, Muslim 1/419.

28. *Subhaanaka Allaahumma wa bihamdika, wa tabaarakasmuka, wa ta'aalaa jadduka, wa laa 'ilaaha ghayruka.*

Glory is to You O Allāh, and praise. Blessed is Your Name and Exalted is Your Majesty. There is none worthy of worship but You.[1]

٢٩-«وَجَّهْتُ وَجْهِيَ لِلَّذِي فَطَرَ السَّمٰوَاتِ وَالأَرْضَ حَنِيفًا وَمَا أَنَا مِنَ الْمُشْرِكِينَ، إِنَّ صَلَاتِي، وَنُسُكِي، وَمَحْيَايَ، وَمَمَاتِي لله رَبِّ الْعَالَمِينَ، لَا شَرِيكَ لَهُ وَبِذَلِكَ أُمِرْتُ وَأَنَا مِنَ الْمُسْلِمِينَ. اللَّهُمَّ أَنْتَ الْمَلِكُ لَا إِلَهَ إِلَّا أَنْتَ. أَنْتَ رَبِّي وَأَنَا عَبْدُكَ، ظَلَمْتُ نَفْسِي وَاعْتَرَفْتُ بِذَنْبِي فَاغْفِرْ لِي ذُنُوبِي جَمِيعًا إِنَّهُ لَا يَغْفِرُ الذُّنُوبَ إِلَّا أَنْتَ. وَاهْدِنِي لِأَحْسَنِ الْأَخْلاقِ

---

[1] Abu Dawud, Ibn Mājah, An-Nasā'i, At-Tirmithi. See Al-Albāni, *Sahih At-Tirmithi* 1/77 and *Sahih Ibn Mājah* 1/135.

لَا يَهْدِي لِأَحْسَنِهَا إِلَّا أَنْتَ، وَاصْرِفْ عَنِّي
سَيِّئَهَا لَا يَصْرِفُ عَنِّي سَيِّئَهَا إِلَّا أَنْتَ، لَبَّيْكَ
وَسَعْدَيْكَ، وَالْخَيْرُ كُلُّهُ بِيَدَيْكَ، وَالشَّرُّ لَيْسَ
إِلَيْكَ، أَنَا بِكَ وَإِلَيْكَ، تَبَارَكْتَ وَتَعَالَيْتَ،
أَسْتَغْفِرُكَ وَأَتُوبُ إِلَيْكَ».

29. Wajjahtu wajhiya lillathee fataras-
samaawaati wal'ardha haneefan wa maa 'anaa
minal-mushrikeen, 'inna salaatee, wa
nusukee, wa mahyaaya, wa mamaatee lillaahi
Rabbil-'aalameen, laa shareeka lahu wa
bithaalika 'umirtu wa 'anaa minal-
muslimeen. Allaahumma 'Antal-Maliku laa
'ilaaha 'illaa 'Anta. 'Anta Rabbee wa 'anaa
'abduka,dhalamtu nafsee wa'taraftu bithanbee
faghfir lee thunoobee jamee'an 'innahu laa
yaghfiruth-thunooba 'illaa 'Anta. Wahdinee
li'ahsanil-'akhlaaqi laa yahdee li'ahsanihaa
'illaa 'Anta, wasrif 'annee sayyi'ahaa, laa
yasrifu 'annee sayyi'ahaa 'illa 'Anta, labbayka
wa sa'dayka, walkhayru kulluhu biyadayka,
washsharru laysa 'ilayka, 'anaa bika wa

'ilayka, tabaarakta wa ta'aalayta, 'astaghfiruka wa 'atoobu 'ilayka.

I turn my face towards the One Who created the heavens and the earth, as a true believer. I am not of those who associate partners with Allāh. Verily, my prayer and my devotion, my living and my death, are for Allāh, Lord of the worlds, He has no partners. Thus I have been commanded and I am among those who have submitted. O Allāh, You are the King, there is none worthy of worship but You. You are my Lord and I am Your slave. I have wronged my own soul and confess my sin. Forgive all of my sins, surely none forgives sins but You. Guide me to the perfection of my character, for none guides to its perfection but You. Protect me from the evils of my character, for none may protect me from its evils but You. I am here at Your service. All goodness is in Your Hands, and evil is not attributed to You. I am (created) by You, and I am (returning) to You. You are Most

Blessed, Most Exalted. I seek Your forgiveness and repent to You.[1]

٣٠-«اللَّهُمَّ رَبَّ جِبْرَائِيلَ، وَمِيكَائِيلَ، وَإِسْرَافِيلَ فَاطِرَ السَّمَوَاتِ وَالْأَرْضِ، عَالِمَ الْغَيْبِ وَالشَّهَادَةِ، أَنْتَ تَحْكُمُ بَيْنَ عِبَادِكَ فِيمَا كَانُوا فِيهِ يَخْتَلِفُونَ. اهْدِنِي لِمَا اخْتُلِفَ فِيهِ مِنَ الْحَقِّ بِإِذْنِكَ إِنَّكَ تَهْدِي مَنْ تَشَاءُ إِلَى صِرَاطٍ مُسْتَقِيمٍ».

30. Allaahumma Rabba Jibraa'eela, wa Mikaa'eela, wa 'Israafeela faatiras-samaawaati wal'ardh, 'Aalimal-ghaybi washshahaadati, 'Anta tahkumu bayna 'ibaadika feemaa kaanoo feehi yakhtalifoon. Ihdinee limakh-tulifa feehi minal-haqqi bi 'ithnika 'innaka tahdee man tashaa'u 'ilaa siraatim-mustaqeem.

O Allāh, Lord of Jibrā'īl, Mikā'īl and Isrāfīl. Maker of the heavens and the earth. Knower of the unseen and the seen. You judge between Your slaves regarding that in which they differ. Guide me to the

---

[1] Muslim 1/534.

49

truth regarding that in which there is difference, by Your leave. Surely, You guide whomever you please to the straight path.[1]

٣١-«اللهُ أَكْبَرُ كَبِيرًا، اللهُ أَكْبَرُ كَبِيرًا، اللهُ أَكْبَرُ كَبِيرًا، وَالْحَمْدُ لِلَّهِ كَثِيرًا، وَالْحَمْدُ لِلَّهِ كَثِيرًا، وَالْحَمْدُ لِلَّهِ كَثِيرًا، وَسُبْحَانَ اللهِ بُكْرَةً وَأَصِيلًا» ثَلَاثًا «أَعُوذُ بِاللهِ مِنَ الشَّيْطَانِ: مِنْ نَفْخِهِ، وَنَفْثِهِ، وَهَمْزِهِ».

31. Allaahu 'Akbar Kabeera, Allaahu 'Akbar Kabeera, Allaahu 'Akbar Kabeera, walhamdu lillaahi katheera, walhamdu lillaahi katheera, walhamdu lillaahi katheera, wa Subhaanallaahi bukratan wa 'aseela. - 'A'oothu billaahi minash-Shaytaan: min nafkhihi, wa nafthihi, wa hamzihi.

Allāh is the Greatest, Most Great. Allāh is the Greatest, Most Great. Allāh is the Greatest, Most Great. Praise is to Allāh,

---

[1] Muslim 1/534.

abundantly. Praise is to Allāh, abundantly. Praise is to Allāh, abundantly. Glory is to Allāh, at the break of day and at its end. [Recite three times in Arabic.] I seek refuge in Allāh from Satan. From his breath and from his voice, and from his whisper.[1]

٣٢-«اللَّهُمَّ لَكَ الْحَمْدُ أَنْتَ نُورُ السَّمَوَاتِ وَالْأَرْضِ وَمَنْ فِيهِنَّ، وَلَكَ الْحَمْدُ أَنْتَ قَيِّمُ السَّمَوَاتِ وَالأَرْضِ وَمَنْ فِيهِنَّ، [وَلَكَ الْحَمْدُ أَنْتَ رَبُّ السَّمَوَاتِ وَالأَرْضِ وَمَنْ فِيهِنَّ] [وَلَكَ الْحَمْدُ لَكَ مُلْكُ السَّمَوَاتِ وَالأَرْضِ وَمَنْ فِيهِنَّ] [وَلَكَ الْحَمْدُ أَنْتَ مَلِكُ السَّمَوَاتِ وَالأَرْضِ] [وَلَكَ الْحَمْدُ] [أَنْتَ الْحَقُّ، وَوَعْدُكَ الْحَقُّ، وَقَوْلُكَ الْحَقُّ، وَلِقَاؤُكَ الْحَقُّ، وَالْجَنَّةُ حَقٌّ، وَالنَّارُ حَقٌّ، وَالنَّبِيُّونَ

[1] Abu Dawud 1/203, Ibn Mājah 1/265, and Ahmad 4/85. Muslim recorded a similar Hadith, 1/420.

حَقٌّ، وَمُحَمَّدٌ ﷺ حَقٌّ، وَالسَّاعَةُ حَقٌّ] [اللَّهُمَّ لَكَ أَسْلَمْتُ، وَعَلَيْكَ تَوَكَّلْتُ، وَبِكَ آمَنْتُ، وَإِلَيْكَ أَنَبْتُ، وَبِكَ خَاصَمْتُ، وَإِلَيْكَ حَاكَمْتُ، فَاغْفِرْ لِي مَا قَدَّمْتُ، وَمَا أَخَّرْتُ، وَمَا أَسْرَرْتُ، وَمَا أَعْلَنْتُ] [أَنْتَ الْمُقَدِّمُ، وَأَنْتَ الْمُؤَخِّرُ لَا إِلَهَ إِلَّا أَنْتَ] [أَنْتَ إِلَهِي لَا إِلَهَ إِلَّا أَنْتَ]».

32. *Allaahumma lakal-hamdu 'Anta noorus-samaawaati wal'ardhi wa man feehinna, wa lakal-hamdu 'Anta qayyimus-samaawaati wal'ardhi wa man feehinna, [wa lakal-hamdu 'Anta Rabbus-samaawaati wal'ardhi wa man feehinna] [wa lakal-hamdu laka mulkus-samaawaati wal'ardhi wa man feehinna] [wa lakal-hamdu 'Anta Malikus-samaawaati wal'ardhi] [wa lakal-hamdu] ['Antal-haqq, wa wa'dukal-haqq, wa qawlukal-haqq wa liqaa'ukal-haqq, waljannatu haqq, wannaaru haqq, wannabiyyoona haqq, wa Muhammadun*

(sallallaahu 'alayhi wa sallam) haqq, wassaa'atu haqq] [Allaahumma laka 'aslamtu, wa 'alayka tawakkaltu, wa bika 'aamantu, wa 'ilayka 'anabtu, wa bika khaasamtu, wa 'ilayka haakamtu. Faghfir lee maa qaddamtu, wa maa 'akhkhartu, wa maa 'asrartu, wa maa 'a'lantu] ['Antal-Muqaddimu, wa 'Antal-Mu'akhkhiru laa 'ilaaha 'illaa 'Anta] ['Anta 'ilaahee laa 'ilaaha 'illaa 'Anta].

O Allāh, praise is to You. You are the Light of the heavens and the earth and all that they contain. Praise is to You, You are the Sustainer of the heavens and the earth and all they contain. [Praise is to You, You are the Lord of the heavens and the earth and all they contain.] [Praise is to You, Yours is dominion of the heavens and the earth and all they contain.] [Praise is to You, You are the King of the heavens and the earth.] [And praise is to You.] [You are the Truth, Your Promise is true, Your Word is true, Your audience is true, Paradise is true, Hell is true, the Prophets are true, and Muhammad (peace and blessings be upon him) is true, and the Hour of Judgment is true.] [O Allāh, to You I have submitted, and upon You I depend. I have believed in You and to You I turn in repentance. For Your sake I dispute and by Your standard I judge. Forgive me what I have sent before me and what I have left behind me, what I have concealed and what I have declared.] [You are the One Who sends forth and You are the One Who delays, there is none who has the right to be worshipped but You.] [You are my God, there is none who has the right to be worshipped but You.][1]

17. Invocations during *Rukū'* (bowing in prayer)

٣٣-«سُبْحَانَ رَبِّيَ الْعَظِيمِ» .

33. *Subhaana Rabbiyal-'Adheem.*

---

[1] Al-Bukhāri, cf. Al-Asqalāni, *Fathul-Bāri* 3/3, 11/116, 13/371, 423, 465. See also Muslim for a shorter account, 1/532.

Glory to my Lord the Exalted (three times in Arabic).[1]

٣٤-«سُبْحَانَكَ اللَّهُمَّ رَبَّنَا وَبِحَمْدِكَ اللَّهُمَّ اغْفِرْ لِي» .

34. *Subhaanaka Allaahumma Rabbanaa wa bihamdika Allaahum-maghfir lee.*

Glory is to You, O Allāh, our Lord, and praise is Yours. O Allāh, forgive me.[2]

٣٥-«سُبُّوحٌ، قُدُّوسٌ، رَبُّ الْمَلَائِكَةِ وَالرُّوحِ» .

35. *Subboohun, Quddoosun, Rabbul-malaa'ikati warrooh.*

Glory (to You), Most Holy (are You), Lord of the angels and the Spirit.[3]

٣٦-«اللَّهُمَّ لَكَ رَكَعْتُ، وَبِكَ آمَنْتُ، وَلَكَ أَسْلَمْتُ خَشَعَ لَكَ سَمْعِي، وَبَصَرِي وَمُخِّي، وَعَظْمِي، وَعَصَبِي، وَمَا اسْتَقَلَّ بِهِ قَدَمِي» .

---

[1] Abu Dawud, Ibn Mājah, An-Nasā'i, At-Tirmithi, and Ahmad. See Al-Albāni's *Sahih At-Tirmithi* 1/83.

[2] Al-Bukhāri 1/99, Muslim 1/350.

[3] Muslim 1/353, Abu Dawud 1/230.

36. *Allaahumma laka raka'tu, wa bika 'aamantu, wa laka 'aslamtu khasha'a laka sam'ee, wa basaree, wa mukhkhee, wa 'adhmee, wa 'asabee, wa mastaqalla bihi qadamee.*

O Allāh, to You I bow (in prayer) and in You I believe and to You I have submitted. Before You my hearing is humbled, as is my sight, my mind, my bones, my nerves and what my feet have mounted upon (for travel).[1]

٣٧-«سُبْحَانَ ذِي الْجَبَرُوتِ، وَالْمَلَكُوتِ، وَالْكِبْرِيَاءِ، وَالْعَظَمَةِ».

37. *Subhaana thil-jabarooti, walmalakooti, walkibriyaa'i, wal'adhamati.*

Glory is to You, Master of power, of dominion, of majesty and greatness.[2]

---

[1] Muslim 1/534, Abu Dawud, An-Nasā'i and At-Tirmithi.

[2] Abu Dawud 1/230, An-Nasā'i and Ahmad. Its chain of narration is good (*Hasan*).

18. Invocations for rising
from the *Rukū'*

٣٨-«سَمِعَ اللهُ لِمَنْ حَمِدَهُ» .

38. Sami'allaahu liman hamidah.

Allāh hears whoever praises Him.[1]

٣٩-رَبَّنَا وَلَكَ الْحَمْدُ، حَمْدًا كَثِيرًا طَيِّبًا مُبَارَكًا فِيهِ» .

39. Rabbanaa wa lakal-hamd, hamdan katheeran tayyiban mubaarakan feeh.

Our Lord, praise is Yours, abundant, good and blessed praise.[2]

٤٠-«مِلْءَ السَّمْوَاتِ وَمِلْءَ الْأَرْضِ وَمَا بَيْنَهُمَا، وَمِلْءَ مَا شِئْتَ مِنْ شَيْءٍ بَعْدُ. أَهْلَ الثَّنَاءِ وَالْمَجْدِ، أَحَقُّ مَا قَالَ الْعَبْدُ، وَكُلُّنَا لَكَ عَبْدٌ. اللَّهُمَّ لَا مَانِعَ لِمَا أَعْطَيْتَ، وَلَا مُعْطِيَ لِمَا مَنَعْتَ، وَلَا يَنْفَعُ ذَالْجَدِّ مِنْكَ الْجَدُّ» .

---

[1] Al-Bukhāri, cf. Al-Asqalāni, *Fathul-Bāri* 2/282.
[2] Al-Bukhāri, cf. Al-Asqalāni, *Fathul-Bāri* 2/284.

40. *Mil'as-samaawaati wa mil'al-'ardhi wa maa baynahumaa, wa mil'a maa shi'ta min shay'in ba'd. 'Ahlath-thanaa'i walmajdi, 'ahaqqu maa qaalal-'abdu, wa kullunaa laka 'abdun. Allaahumma laa maani'a limaa 'a'tayta, wa laa mu'tiya limaa mana'ta, wa laa yanfa'u thal-jaddi minkal-jadd.*

(A praise that) fills the heavens and the earth and what lies between them, and whatever else You please. (You Allāh) are most worthy of praise and majesty, and what the slave has said – we are all Your slaves. O Allāh, there is none who can withhold what You give, and none may give what You have withheld. And the might of the mighty person cannot benefit him against You.[1]

19. Invocations during *Sujood*

٤١ -«سُبْحَانَ رَبِّيَ الأَعْلَى».

41. *Subhaana Rabbiyal-A'laa.*

Glory is to my Lord, the Most High. (This

---

[1] Muslim 1/346.

is said three times in Arabic.)[1]

٤٢ –«سُبْحَانَكَ اللَّهُمَّ رَبَّنَا وَبِحَمْدِكَ اللَّهُمَّ اغْفِرْ
لِي» .

42. *Subhaanaka Allaahumma Rabbanaa wa bihamdika Allaahum-maghfir lee.*

Glory is to You, O Allāh, our Lord, and praise is Yours. O Allāh, forgive me.[2]

٤٣ –«سُبُّوحٌ، قُدُّوسٌ، رَبُّ الْمَلَائِكَةِ وَالرُّوحِ» .

43. *Subboohun, Quddoosun, Rabbul-malaa'ikati warrooh.*

Glory (to You), Most Holy (are You), Lord of the angels and the Spirit.[3]

٤٤ –«اللَّهُمَّ لَكَ سَجَدْتُ وَبِكَ آمَنْتُ، وَلَكَ
أَسْلَمْتُ، سَجَدَ وَجْهِيَ لِلَّذِي خَلَقَهُ، وَصَوَّرَهُ،

---

[1] Abu Dawud, Ibn Mājah, An-Nasā'i, At-Tirmithi, and Ahmad. See also Al-Albāni, *Sahih At-Tirmithi* 1/83.

[2] Al-Bukhāri and Muslim, see invocation no. 34 above.

[3] Muslim 1/533, see invocation no. 35 above.

وَشَقَّ سَمْعَهُ وَبَصَرَهُ، تَبَارَكَ اللهُ أَحْسَنُ الْخَالِقِينَ».

44. *Allaahumma laka sajadtu wa bika 'aamantu, wa laka 'aslamtu, sajada wajhiya lillathee khalaqahu, wa sawwarahu, wa shaqqa sam'ahu wa basarahu, tabaarakallaahu 'ahsanul-khaaliqeen.*

O Allāh, to You I prostrate myself and in You I believe. To You I have submitted. My face is prostrated to the One Who created it, fashioned it, and gave it hearing and sight. Blessed is Allāh, the Best of creators.[1]

٤٥ -«سُبْحَانَ ذِي الْجَبَرُوتِ، وَالْمَلَكُوتِ، وَالْكِبْرِيَاءِ، وَالْعَظَمَةِ».

45. *Subhaana thil-jabarooti, walmalakooti, walkibriyaa'i, wal'adhamati.*

Glory is to You, Master of power, of dominion, of majesty and greatness.[2]

---

[1] Muslim 1/534 and others.

[2] Abu Dawud 1/230, An-Nasā'i, Ahmad. See

٤٦-«اللَّهُمَّ اغْفِرْ لِي ذَنْبِي كُلَّهُ، دِقَّهُ وَجِلَّهُ، وَأَوَّلَهُ وَآخِرَهُ وَعَلَانِيَتَهُ وَسِرَّهُ»

46. Allaahum-maghfir lee thanbee kullahu, diqqahu wa jillahu, wa 'awwalahu wa 'aakhirahu wa 'alaaniyatahu wa sirrahu.

O Allāh, forgive me all my sins, great and small, the first and the last, those that are apparent and those that are hidden.[1]

٤٧-«اللَّهُمَّ إِنِّي أَعُوذُ بِرِضَاكَ مِنْ سَخَطِكَ، وَبِمُعَافَاتِكَ مِنْ عُقُوبَتِكَ، وَأَعُوذُ بِكَ مِنْكَ، لَا أُحْصِي ثَنَاءً عَلَيْكَ أَنْتَ كَمَا أَثْنَيْتَ عَلَى نَفْسِكَ».

47. Allaahumma 'innee 'a'oothu biridhaaka min sakhatika, wa bimu'aafaatika min 'uqoobatika wa 'a'oothu bika minka, laa 'uhsee thanaa'an 'alayka 'Anta kamaa 'athnayta 'alaa nafsika.

O Allāh, I seek protection in Your

also Al-Albāni, *Sahih Abu Dawud* 1/166, see invocation no. 37 above.
[1] Muslim 1/350.

pleasure from Your anger, and I seek protection in Your forgiveness from Your punishment. I seek protection in You from You. I cannot count Your praises. You are as You have praised Yourself.[1]

20. Invocations for sitting between two prostrations

٤٨-«رَبِّ اغْفِرْ لِي رَبِّ اغْفِرْ لِي» .

48. *Rabbighfir lee, Rabbighfir lee.*

My Lord, forgive me. My Lord, forgive me.[2]

٤٩-«اللَّهُمَّ اغْفِرْ لِي، وَارْحَمْنِي، وَاهْدِنِي، وَاجْبُرْنِي، وَعَافِنِي، وَارْزُقْنِي، وَارْفَعْنِي» .

49. *Allaahum-maghfir lee, warhamnee, wahdinee, wajburnee, wa 'aafinee, warzuqnee, warfa'nee.*

O Allāh forgive me, have mercy on me,

---

[1] Muslim 1/352.
[2] Abu Dawud 1/231. See also Al-Albāni, *Sahih Ibn Mājah* 1/148.

guide me, support me, protect me, provide for me and elevate me.[1]

21. Supplications for prostrating due to recitation of the Qur'ān

٥٠-«سَجَدَ وَجْهِيَ لِلَّذِي خَلَقَهُ، وَشَقَّ سَمْعَهُ وَبَصَرَهُ، بِحَوْلِهِ وَقُوَّتِهِ، فَتَبَارَكَ اللهُ أَحْسَنُ الْخَالِقِينَ».

50. *Sajada wajhiya lillathee khalaqahu, wa shaqqa sam'ahu wa basarahu bihawlihi wa quwwatihi. Fatabaarakallaahu 'ahsanul-khaaliqeen.*

I have prostrated my face to the One Who created it, and gave it hearing and sight by His might and His power. Glory is to Allāh, the Best of creators.[2]

---

[1] Abu Dawud, Ibn Mājah, At-Tirmithi. See also Al-Albāni, *Sahih At-Tirmithi* 1/90 and *Sahih Ibn Mājah* 1/148.

[2] At-Tirmithi 2/474, Ahmad 6/30, and Al-Hākim who graded it authentic and Ath-Thahabi agreed with him 1/220.

٥١-«اللَّهُمَّ اكْتُبْ لِي بِهَا عِنْدَكَ أَجْرًا، وَضَعْ
عَنِّي بِهَا وِزْرًا، وَاجْعَلْهَا لِي عِنْدَكَ ذُخْرًا،
وَتَقَبَّلْهَا مِنِّي كَمَا تَقَبَّلْتَهَا مِنْ عَبْدِكَ دَاوُدَ»

51. *Allaahum-maktub lee bihaa 'indaka
'ajran, wa dha' 'annee bihaa wizran,
waj'alhaa lee 'indaka thukhran, wa
taqabbalhaa minnee kamaa taqabbaltahaa min
'abdika Daawooda.*

O Allāh, write it as a reward for me, and
release me from a burden for it, and make
it a treasure for me in Paradise. Accept it
from me as You accepted it from your
servant Dāwud.[1]

22. Invocation for *At-Tashahhud*
(sitting in prayer)

٥٢-«التَّحِيَّاتُ لله، وَالصَّلَوَاتُ، وَالطَّيِّبَاتُ،
السَّلَامُ عَلَيْكَ أَيُّهَا النَّبِيُّ وَرَحْمَةُ اللهِ وَبَرَكَاتُهُ،

---

[1] At-Tirmithi 2/473, and Al-Hākim who
graded it authentic and Ath-Thahabi agreed
1/219.

السَّلَامُ عَلَيْنَا وَعَلَى عِبَادِ اللهِ الصَّالِحِينَ . أَشْهَدُ
أَنْ لَا إِلَهَ إِلَّا اللهُ وَأَشْهَدُ أَنَّ مُحَمَّدًا عَبْدُهُ
وَرَسُولُهُ﴾

52. *Attahiyyaatu lillaahi wassalawaatu, wattayyibaatu, assalaamu 'alayka 'ayyuhan-Nabiyyu wa rahmatullaahi wa barakaatuhu, assalaamu 'alaynaa wa 'alaa 'ibaadillaahis-saaliheen. 'Ash-hadu 'an laa 'ilaaha 'illallaahu wa 'ash-hadu 'anna Muhammadan 'abduhu wa Rasooluhu.*

All greetings of humility are for Allāh, and all prayers and goodness. Peace be upon you, O Prophet, and the mercy of Allāh and His blessings. Peace be upon us and upon the righteous slaves of Allāh. I bear witness that there is none worthy of worship but Allāh, and I bear witness that Muhammad is His slave and His Messenger.[1]

---

[1] Al-Bukhāri, Muslim 1/301. See also Al-Asqalāni, *Fathul-Bāri* 1/13.

23. How to recite blessings on the Prophet after the *Tashahhud*

٥٣- «اللَّهُمَّ صَلِّ عَلَى مُحَمَّدٍ وَعَلَى آلِ مُحَمَّدٍ،
كَمَا صَلَّيْتَ عَلَى إِبْرَاهِيمَ وَعَلَى آلِ إِبْرَاهِيمَ،
إِنَّكَ حَمِيدٌ مَجِيدٌ، اللَّهُمَّ بَارِكْ عَلَى مُحَمَّدٍ
وَعَلَى آلِ مُحَمَّدٍ كَمَا بَارَكْتَ عَلَى إِبْرَاهِيمَ
وَعَلَى آلِ إِبْرَاهِيمَ، إِنَّكَ حَمِيدٌ مَجِيدٌ».

53. *Allaahumma salli 'alaa Muhammadin wa 'alaa 'aali Muhammadin, kamaa sallayta 'alaa 'Ibraaheema wa 'alaa 'aali 'Ibraaheema, 'innaka Hameedun Majeed. Allaahumma baarik 'alaa Muhammadin wa 'alaa 'aali Muhammadin, kamaa baarakta 'alaa 'Ibraaheema wa 'alaa 'aali 'Ibraaheema, 'innaka Hameedun Majeed.*

O Allāh, bestow Your favor on Muhammad and on the family of Muhammad as You have bestowed Your favor on Ibrahim and on the family of Ibrahim, You are Praiseworthy, Most

Glorious. O Allāh, bless Muhammad and the family of Muhammad as You have blessed Ibrahim and the family of Ibrahim, You are Praiseworthy, Most Glorious.[1]

٥٤ – «اللَّهُمَّ صَلِّ عَلَى مُحَمَّدٍ وَعَلَى أَزْوَاجِهِ وَذُرِّيَّتِهِ، كَمَا صَلَّيْتَ عَلَى آلِ إِبْرَاهِيمَ، وَبَارِكْ عَلَى مُحَمَّدٍ وَعَلَى أَزْوَاجِهِ وَذُرِّيَّتِهِ، كَمَا بَارَكْتَ عَلَى آلِ إِبْرَاهِيمَ، إِنَّكَ حَمِيدٌ مَجِيدٌ».

54. *Allaahumma salli 'alaa Muhammadin wa 'alaa 'azwaajihi wa thurriyyatihi, kamaa sallayta 'alaa 'aali 'Ibraaheema. Wa baarik 'alaa Muhammadin wa 'alaa 'azwaajihi wa thurriyyatihi, kamaa baarakta 'alaa 'aali 'Ibraaheema. 'Innaka Hameedun Majeed.*

O Allāh, bestow Your favor on Muhammad and upon his wives and progeny as You have bestowed Your favor upon the family of Ibrahim. And bless Muhammad and his wives and

---

[1] Al-Bukhāri, cf. Al-Asqalāni, *Fathul-Bāri* 6/408.

progeny as You have blessed the family of Ibrahim, You are full of praise, Most Glorious.[1]

24. Invocations after the final *Tashahhud* and before ending the prayer

٥٥-«اللَّهُمَّ إِنِّي أَعُوذُ بِكَ مِنْ عَذَابِ الْقَبْرِ، وَمِنْ عَذَابِ جَهَنَّمَ، وَمِنْ فِتْنَةِ الْمَحْيَا وَالْمَمَاتِ، وَمِنْ شَرِّ فِتْنَةِ الْمَسِيحِ الدَّجَّالِ».

55. *Allaahumma 'innee 'a'oothu bika min 'athaabil-qabri, wa min 'athaabi jahannama, wa min fitnatil-mahyaa walmamaati, wa min sharri fitnatil-maseehid-dajjaal.*

O Allāh, I seek refuge in You from the punishment of the grave, and from the punishment of Hell-fire, and from the trials of life and death, and from the evil of the trial of the False Messiah.[2]

---

[1] Al-Bukhāri, from Al-Asqalāni, *Fathul-Bāri* 6/407, Muslim 1/306.

[2] Al-Bukhāri 2/102, Muslim 1/412, and this is Muslim's wording.

٥٦- «اللَّهُمَّ إِنِّي أَعُوذُ بِكَ مِنْ عَذَابِ الْقَبْرِ، وَأَعُوذُ بِكَ مِنْ فِتْنَةِ الْمَسِيحِ الدَّجَّالِ، وَأَعُوذُ بِكَ مِنْ فِتْنَةِ الْمَحْيَا وَالْمَمَاتِ. اللَّهُمَّ إِنِّي أَعُوذُ بِكَ مِنَ الْمَأْثَمِ وَالْمَغْرَمِ».

56. Allaahumma 'innee 'a'oothu bika min 'athaabil-qabri, wa 'a'oothu bika min fitnatil-maseehid-dajjaali, wa 'a'oothu bika min fitnatil-mahyaa walmamaati. Allaahumma 'innee 'a'oothu bika minal-ma'thami walmaghrami.

O Allāh, I seek refuge in You from the punishment of the grave, and I seek refuge in You from the trial of the False Messiah, and I seek refuge in You from the trials of life and death. O Allāh, I seek refuge in You from sin and from debt.[1]

٥٧- «اللَّهُمَّ إِنِّي ظَلَمْتُ نَفْسِي ظُلْمًا كَثِيرًا، وَلَا يَغْفِرُ الذُّنُوبَ إِلَّا أَنْتَ، فَاغْفِرْلِي مَغْفِرَةً مِنْ

---

[1] Al-Bukhāri 1/202, Muslim 1/412.

عِنْدِكَ وَارْحَمْنِي إِنَّكَ أَنْتَ الْغَفُورُ الرَّحِيمُ».

57. Allaahumma 'innee dhalamtu nafsee dhulman katheeran, wa laa yaghfiruth-thunooba 'illaa 'Anta, faghfir lee maghfiratan min 'indika warhamnee 'innaka 'Antal-Ghafoorur-Raheem.

O Allāh, I have greatly wronged myself and no one forgives sins but You. So, grant me forgiveness and have mercy on me. Surely, You are Forgiving, Merciful.[1]

٥٨-«اللَّهُمَّ اغْفِرْ لِي مَا قَدَّمْتُ، وَمَا أَخَّرْتُ، وَمَا أَسْرَرْتُ، وَمَا أَعْلَنْتُ، وَمَا أَسْرَفْتُ، وَمَا أَنْتَ أَعْلَمُ بِهِ مِنِّي. أَنْتَ الْمُقَدِّمُ، وَأَنْتَ الْمُؤَخِّرُ لَا إِلَهَ إِلَّا أَنْتَ».

58. Allaahum-maghfir lee maa qaddamtu, wa maa 'akhkhartu, wa maa 'asrartu, wa maa 'a'lantu, wa maa 'asraftu, wa maa 'Anta 'a'lamu bihi minnee. 'Antal-Muqaddimu, wa

---

[1] Al-Bukhāri 8/168, Muslim 4/2078.

70

'Antal-Mu'akhkhiru laa 'ilaaha 'illaa 'Anta.

O Allāh, forgive me what I have sent before me and what I have left behind me, what I have concealed and what I have done openly, what I have done in excess, and what You are better aware of than I. You are the One Who sends forth and You are the One Who delays. There is none worthy of worship but You.[1]

٥٩- «اللَّهُمَّ أَعِنِّي عَلَى ذِكْرِكَ، وَشُكْرِكَ، وَحُسْنِ عِبَادَتِكَ» .

59. *Allaahumma 'a'innee 'alaa thikrika, wa shukrika, wa husni 'ibaadatika.*

O Allāh, help me to remember You, to give You thanks, and to perform Your worship in the best manner.[2]

٦٠- «اللَّهُمَّ إِنِّي أَعُوذُ بِكَ مِنَ الْبُخْلِ، وَأَعُوذُ بِكَ مِنَ الْجُبْنِ، وَأَعُوذُ بِكَ مِنْ أَنْ أُرَدَّ إِلَى

---

[1] Muslim 1/534.

[2] Abu Dawud 2/86, An-Nasā'i 3/53. See also Al-Albāni *Sahih Abu Dawud* 1/284.

أَرْذَلِ الْعُمُرِ، وَأَعُوذُ بِكَ مِنْ فِتْنَةِ الدُّنْيَا وَعَذَابِ الْقَبْرِ».

60. *Allaahumma 'innee 'a'oothu bika minal-bukhli, wa 'a'oothu bika minal-jubni, wa 'a'oothu bika min 'an 'uradda 'ilaa 'arthalil-'umuri, wa 'a'oothu bika min fitnatid-dunyaa wa 'athaabil-qabri.*

O Allāh, I seek Your protection from miserliness, I seek Your protection from cowardice, and I seek Your protection from being returned to feeble old age. I seek Your protection from the trials of this world and from the torment of the grave.[1]

٦١ –«اللَّهُمَّ إِنِّي أَسْأَلُكَ الْجَنَّةَ وَأَعُوذُ بِكَ مِنَ النَّارِ».

61. *Allaahumma 'innee 'as'alukal-jannata wa 'a'oothu bika minan-naar.*

O Allāh, I ask You for Paradise and seek

---

[1] Al-Bukhāri, cf. Al-Asqalāni, *Fathul-Bāri* 6/35.

Your protection from the Fire.[1]

٦٢-"اللَّهُمَّ بِعِلْمِكَ الْغَيْبَ وَقُدْرَتِكَ عَلَى
الْخَلْقِ أَحْيِنِي مَا عَلِمْتَ الْحَيَاةَ خَيْرًا لِي
وَتَوَفَّنِي إِذَا عَلِمْتَ الْوَفَاةَ خَيْرًا لِي، اللَّهُمَّ إِنِّي
أَسْأَلُكَ خَشْيَتَكَ فِي الْغَيْبِ وَالشَّهَادَةِ،
وَأَسْأَلُكَ كَلِمَةَ الْحَقِّ فِي الرِّضَا وَالْغَضَبِ،
وَأَسْأَلُكَ الْقَصْدَ فِي الْغِنَى وَالْفَقْرِ، وَأَسْأَلُكَ
نَعِيمًا لَا يَنْفَدُ، وَأَسْأَلُكَ قُرَّةَ عَيْنٍ لَا تَنْقَطِعُ،
وَأَسْأَلُكَ الرِّضَا بَعْدَ الْقَضَاءِ، وَأَسْأَلُكَ بَرْدَ
الْعَيْشِ بَعْدَ الْمَوْتِ، وَأَسْأَلُكَ لَذَّةَ النَّظَرِ إِلَى
وَجْهِكَ وَالشَّوْقَ إِلَى لِقَائِكَ فِي غَيْرِ ضَرَّاءَ
مُضِرَّةٍ وَلَا فِتْنَةٍ مُضِلَّةٍ، اللَّهُمَّ زَيِّنَّا بِزِينَةِ الْإِيمَانِ
وَاجْعَلْنَا هُدَاةً مُهْتَدِينَ» .

62. *Allaahumma bi'ilmikal-ghayba wa*

***

[1] Abu Dawud. See also Al-Albāni, *Sahih Ibn
Mājah* 2/328.

qudratika 'alal-khalqi 'ahyinee maa 'alimtal-hayaata khayran lee wa tawaffanee 'ithaa 'alimtal-wafaata khayran lee, Allaahumma 'innee 'as'aluka khashyataka fil-ghaybi wash-shahaadati, wa 'as'aluka kalimatal-haqqi fir-ridhaa walghadhabi, wa 'as'alukal-qasda fil-ghinaa walfaqri, wa 'as'aluka na'eeman laa yanfadu, wa 'as'aluka qurrata 'aynin laa tanqati'u, wa 'as'alukar-ridhaa ba'dal-qadhaa'i, wa 'as'aluka bardal-'ayshi ba'dal-mawti, wa 'as'aluka laththatan-nadhari 'ilaa wajhika wash-shawqa 'ilaa liqaa'ika fee ghayri dharraa'a mudhirratin wa laa fitnatin mudhillatin, Allaahumma zayyinnaa bizeenatil-'eemaani waj'alnaa hudaatan muhtadeen.

O Allāh, by Your Knowledge of the unseen and by Your Power over creation, let me live if You know that life is good for me, and let me die if You know that death is good for me. O Allāh, I ask You to grant me fear of You in private and in public. I ask you for the word of truth in times of contentment and anger. I ask

74

You for moderation in wealth and in poverty. I ask you for blessings never ceasing and the coolness of my eye (i.e. pleasure) that never ends. I ask You for pleasure after Your Judgment and I ask You for a life of coolness after death. I ask You for the delight of gazing upon Your Face and the joy of meeting You without any harm and misleading trials befalling me. O Allāh, dress us with the beauty of Faith, and make us guides who are upon (correct) guidance.[1]

٦٣ –«اللَّهُمَّ إِنِّي أَسْأَلُكَ يَا اللهُ بِأَنَّكَ الْوَاحِدُ الْأَحَدُ الصَّمَدُ الَّذِي لَمْ يَلِدْ وَلَمْ يُولَدْ وَلَمْ يَكُنْ لَهُ كُفُوًا أَحَدٌ، أَنْ تَغْفِرَ لِي ذُنُوبِي إِنَّكَ أَنْتَ الْغَفُورُ الرَّحِيمُ».

63. *Allaahumma 'innee 'as'aluka yaa Allaahu bi'annakal-Waahidul-'Ahadus-Samadul-lathee, lam yalid wa lam yoolad, wa lam*

---

[1] An-Nasā'i 3/54, 55, Ahmad 4/364. See also Al-Albāni, *Sahih An-Nasā'i* 1/281.

yakun lahu kufuwan 'Ahad, 'an taghfira lee thunoobee 'innaka 'Antal-Ghafoorur-Raheem.

O Allāh, I ask You. O Allāh, You are the One, the Only, Self-Sufficient Master, Who was not begotten and begets not and none is equal to Him. Forgive me my sins, surely you are Forgiving, Merciful.[1]

٦٤-«اللَّهُمَّ إِنِّي أَسْأَلُكَ بِأَنَّ لَكَ الْحَمْدَ لَا إِلَهَ إِلَّا أَنْتَ وَحْدَكَ لَا شَرِيكَ لَكَ، الْمَنَّانُ، يَا بَدِيعَ السَّمَوَاتِ وَالْأَرْضِ يَا ذَا الْجَلَالِ وَالْإِكْرَامِ، يَاحَيُّ يَاقَيُّومُ إِنِّي أَسْأَلُكَ الْجَنَّةَ وَأَعُوذُ بِكَ مِنَ النَّارِ».

64. *Allaahumma 'innee 'as'aluka bi'anna lakal-hamda laa 'ilaaha 'illaa 'Anta wahdaka laa shareeka laka, Al-Mannaanu, yaa Badee'as-samaawaati wal'ardhi yaa Thal-Jalaali wal-'Ikraam, yaa Hayyu yaa*

---

[1] An-Nasā'i 3/52, Ahmad 4/338. See also Al-Albāni, *Sahih An-Nasā'i* 1/280 and *Sifat Salātun-Nabi*, pg. 204.

Qayyoomu 'innee 'as'alukal-jannata wa 'a'oothu bika minan-naar.

O Allāh, I ask You, as You are the Owner of praise, there is none worthy of worship but You alone, You have no partner. You are the Giver of all good. O Creator of the heavens and the earth, Owner of majesty and honor. O Living and Everlasting One, I ask you for Paradise and I seek refuge in You from the Fire.[1]

٦٥-«اللَّهُمَّ إِنِّي أَسْأَلُكَ بِأَنِّي أَشْهَدُ أَنَّكَ أَنْتَ اللهُ لَا إِلَهَ إِلَّا أَنْتَ الْأَحَدُ الصَّمَدُ الَّذِي لَمْ يَلِدْ وَلَمْ يُولَدْ وَلَمْ يَكُنْ لَهُ كُفُوًا أَحَدٌ».

65. *Allaahumma 'innee 'as'aluka bi'annee 'ash-hadu 'annaka 'Antallaahu laa 'ilaaha 'illaa 'Antal-'Ahadus-Samadul-lathee lam yalid wa lam yoolad wa lam yakun lahu kufuwan 'Ahad.*

---

[1] Abu Dawud, An-Nasā'i, Ibn Mājah, At-Tirmithi. See also Al-Albāni, *Sahih Ibn Mājah* 2/329.

O Allāh, I ask You, by the fact that I bear witness that You are Allāh. There is none worthy of worship but You, the Only God, Independent of creation, Who was not begotten and begets not, and none is equal to Him.[1]

25. What to say after completing the prayer

٦٥-«أَسْتَغْفِرُ اللهَ (ثَلَاثًا) اللَّهُمَّ أَنْتَ السَّلَامُ وَمِنْكَ السَّلَامُ، تَبَارَكْتَ يَا ذَا الْجَلَالِ وَالْإِكْرَامِ».

66. 'Astaghfirullaaha Allaahumma 'Antas-Salaamu wa minkas-salaamu, tabaarakta yaa Thal-Jalaali wal-'Ikraam.

I seek the forgiveness of Allāh (three times). O Allāh, You are Peace and from You comes peace. Blessed are You, O

---

[1] Abu Dawud 2/62, Ibn Mājah 2/1267, At-Tirmithi 5/515, Ahmad 5/360. See also Al-Albāni, Sahih Ibn Mājah 2/329 and Sahih At-Tirmithi 3/163.

Owner of majesty and honor.[1]

٦٧-«لَا إِلَهَ إِلَّا اللهُ وَحْدَهُ لَا شَرِيكَ لَهُ، لَهُ الْمُلْكُ وَلَهُ الْحَمْدُ وَهُوَ عَلَى كُلِّ شَيْءٍ قَدِيرٌ، اللَّهُمَّ لَا مَانِعَ لِمَا أَعْطَيْتَ، وَلَا مُعْطِيَ لِمَا مَنَعْتَ، وَلَا يَنْفَعُ ذَا الْجَدِّ مِنْكَ الْجَدُّ».

67. Laa 'ilaaha 'illallaahu wahdahu laa shareeka lahu, lahul-mulku wa lahul-hamdu wa Huwa 'alaa kulli shay'in Qadeer, Allaahumma laa maani'a limaa 'a'tayta, wa laa mu'tiya limaa mana'ta, wa laa yanfa'u thal-jaddi minkal-jadd.

None has the right to be worshipped but Allāh alone, He has no partner, His is the dominion and His is the praise, and He is Able to do all things. O Allāh, there is none who can withhold what You give, and none may give what You have withheld; and the might of the mighty person cannot benefit him against You.[2]

---

[1] Muslim 1/414.

[2] Al-Bukhāri 1/255, Muslim 1/414.

٦٨-«لَا إِلَهَ إِلَّا اللهُ وَحْدَهُ لَا شَرِيكَ لَهُ، لَهُ الْمُلْكُ وَلَهُ الْحَمْدُ وَهُوَ عَلَى كُلِّ شَيْءٍ قَدِيرٌ، لَا حَوْلَ وَلَا قُوَّةَ إِلَّا بِاللهِ، لَا إِلَهَ إِلَّا اللهُ، وَلَا نَعْبُدُ إِلَّا إِيَّاهُ، لَهُ النِّعْمَةُ وَلَهُ الْفَضْلُ وَلَهُ الثَّنَاءُ الْحَسَنُ، لَا إِلَهَ إِلَّا اللهُ مُخْلِصِينَ لَهُ الدِّينَ وَلَوْ كَرِهَ الْكَافِرُونَ».

68. Laa 'ilaaha 'illallaahu wahdahu laa shareeka lahu, lahul-mulku, wa lahul-hamdu wa Huwa 'alaa kulli shay'in Qadeer. Laa hawla wa laa quwwata 'illaa billaahi, laa 'ilaaha 'illallaahu, wa laa na'budu 'illaa 'iyyaahu, lahun-ni'matu wa lahul-fadhlu wa lahuth-thanaa'ul-hasanu, laa 'ilaaha 'illallaahu mukhliseena lahud-deena wa law karihal-kaafiroon.

None has the right to be worshipped but Allāh alone, He has no partner, His is the dominion and His is the praise and He is Able to do all things. There is no power and no might except by Allāh. None has

the right to be worshipped but Allāh, and
we do not worship any other besides
Him. His is grace, and His is bounty and
to Him belongs the most excellent praise.
None has the right to be worshipped but
Allāh. (We are) sincere in making our
religious devotion to Him, even though
the disbelievers may dislike it.[1]

٦٩ -«سُبْحَانَ اللهِ، وَالْحَمْدُ للهِ، وَاللهُ أَكْبَرُ
(ثَلَاثًا وَثَلَاثِينَ) لَا إِلَهَ إِلَّا اللهُ وَحْدَهُ لَا شَرِيكَ
لَهُ، لَهُ الْمُلْكُ وَلَهُ الْحَمْدُ وَهُوَ عَلَى كُلِّ شَيْءٍ
قَدِيرٌ» .

69. Subhaanallaahi, walhamdu lillaahi
wallaahu 'Akbar, – Laa 'ilaaha 'illallaahu
wahdahu laa shareeka lahu, lahul-mulku wa
lahul-hamdu wa Huwa 'alaa kulli shay'in
Qadeer.

Glory is to Allāh, and praise is to Allāh,
and Allāh is the Most Great (each said
thirty-three times). None has the right to

[1] Muslim 1/415.

be worshipped but Allāh alone, He has no partner, His is the dominion and His is the praise and He is Able to do all things.[1]

٧٠- بِسۡمِ ٱللَّهِ ٱلرَّحۡمَٰنِ ٱلرَّحِيمِ ﴿قُلۡ هُوَ ٱللَّهُ أَحَدٌ ۝ ٱللَّهُ ٱلصَّمَدُ ۝ لَمۡ يَلِدۡ وَلَمۡ يُولَدۡ ۝ وَلَمۡ يَكُن لَّهُۥ كُفُوًا أَحَدُۢ ﴾

70. Bismillaahir-Rahmaanir-Raheem. Qul Huwallaahu 'Ahad. Allaahus-Samad. Lam yalid wa lam yoolad. Wa lam yakun lahu kufuwan 'ahad.

With the Name of Allāh, the Most Gracious, the Most Merciful. Say: He is Allāh (the) One. The Self-Sufficient Master, Whom all creatures need, He begets not nor was He begotten, and there is none equal to Him.[2]

---

[1] Muslim 1/418, Whoever says this after every prayer will be forgiven his sins even though they be as the foam of the sea.
[2] Al-Ikhlās 112:1-4.

بِسْمِ اللهِ الرَّحْمَنِ الرَّحِيمِ ﴿قُلْ أَعُوذُ بِرَبِّ
الْفَلَقِ ٥ مِن شَرِّ مَا خَلَقَ ٥ وَمِن شَرِّ غَاسِقٍ إِذَا وَقَبَ
٥ وَمِن شَرِّ النَّفَّثَتِ فِى الْعُقَدِ ٥وَمِن شَرِّ حَاسِدٍ إِذَا
حَسَدَ ﴾

*Bismillaahir-Rahmaanir-Raheem. Qul
'a'oothu birabbil-falaq. Min sharri maa
khalaq. Wa min sharri ghaasiqin 'ithaa waqab.
Wa min sharrin-naffaathaati fil-'uqad. Wa
min sharri haasidin 'ithaa hasad.*

With the Name of Allāh, the Most
Gracious, the Most Merciful. Say: I seek
refuge with (Allāh) the Lord of the
daybreak, from the evil of what He has
created, and from the evil of the
darkening (night) as it comes with its
darkness, and from the evil of those who
practice witchcraft when they blow in the
knots, and from the evil of the envier
when he envies.[1]

بِسْمِ اللهِ الرَّحْمَنِ الرَّحِيمِ ﴿قُلْ أَعُوذُ بِرَبِّ

[1] Al-Falaq 113:1-5.

83

أَلنَّاسِ ٥ مَلِكِ ٱلنَّاسِ ٥ إِلَهِ ٱلنَّاسِ ٥ مِن شَرِّ
ٱلْوَسْوَاسِ ٱلْخَنَّاسِ ٥ ٱلَّذِى يُوَسْوِسُ فِى صُدُورِ ٱلنَّاسِ
٥ مِنَ ٱلْجِنَّةِ وَٱلنَّاسِ ﴾ .

*Bismillaahir-Rahmaanir-Raheem. Qul
'a'oothu birabbin-naas. Malikin-naas.
'Ilaahin-naas. Min sharril-waswaasil-
khannaas. Allathee yuwaswisu fee sudoorin-
naas. Minal-jinnati wannaas.*

With the Name of Allāh, the Most
Gracious, the Most Merciful. Say: I seek
refuge with (Allāh) the Lord of mankind,
the King of mankind, the God of
mankind, from the evil of the whisperer
who withdraws, who whispers in the
breasts of mankind, of jinns and men.[1]
(These *Surahs* should be recited in Arabic
after each prayer. After the *Maghrib* and
Fajr prayers they should be recited three
times each.)[2]

---

[1] *An-Nās* 114:1-6.
[2] Abu Dawud 2/86, An-Nasā'i 3/68. See also
Al-Albāni, *Sahih At-Tirmithi* 2/8.

٧١- ۞اللَّهُ لَا إِلَـٰهَ إِلَّا هُوَ الْحَيُّ الْقَيُّومُ لَا تَأْخُذُهُ
سِنَةٌ وَلَا نَوْمٌ لَّهُ مَا فِي السَّمَوَاتِ وَمَا فِي الْأَرْضِ مَن
ذَا الَّذِي يَشْفَعُ عِندَهُ إِلَّا بِإِذْنِهِ يَعْلَمُ مَا بَيْنَ
أَيْدِيهِمْ وَمَا خَلْفَهُمْ وَلَا يُحِيطُونَ بِشَيْءٍ مِّنْ عِلْمِهِ
إِلَّا بِمَا شَاءَ وَسِعَ كُرْسِيُّهُ السَّمَوَاتِ وَالْأَرْضَ وَلَا
يَئُودُهُ حِفْظُهُمَا وَهُوَ الْعَلِيُّ الْعَظِيمُ ۞.

71. Allaahu laa 'ilaaha 'illaa Huwal-Hayyul-
Qayyoom, laa ta'khuthuhu sinatun wa laa
nawm, lahu maa fis-samaawaati wa maa fil-
'ardh, man thal-lathee yashfa'u 'indahu 'illaa
bi'ithnih, ya'lamu maa bayna 'aydeehim wa
maa khalfahum, wa laa yuheetoona bishay'im-
min 'ilmihi 'illaa bimaa shaa'a, wasi'a
kursiyyuhus-samaawaati wal'ardh, wa laa
ya'ooduhu hifdhuhumaa, wa Huwal-'Aliyyul-
'Adheem.

Allāh! There is none worthy of worship
but He, the Ever Living, the One Who
sustains and protects all that exists.
Neither slumber nor sleep overtakes Him.

To Him belongs whatever is in the heavens and whatever is on the earth. Who is he that can intercede with Him except with His Permission? He knows what happens to them in this world, and what will happen to them in the Hereafter. And they will never compass anything of His Knowledge except that which He wills. His Throne extends over the heavens and the earth, and He feels no fatigue in guarding and preserving them. And He is the Most High, the Most Great. (Recite in Arabic after each prayer.)[1]

٧٢-«لَا إِلٰهَ إِلَّا اللهُ وَحْدَهُ لَا شَرِيكَ لَهُ، لَهُ الْمُلْكُ وَلَهُ الْحَمْدُ يُحْيِي وَيُمِيتُ، وَهُوَ عَلَى كُلِّ شَيْءٍ قَدِيرٌ».

72. Laa 'ilaaha 'illallaahu wahdahu laa shareeka lahu, lahul-mulku wa lahul-hamdu

[1] An-Nasā'i, 'Amalul-Yawm wal-Laylah (Hadith no. 100), also Ibn As-Sunni (no. 121). See also Al-Albāni, Sahihul-Jāmi' As-Saghīr 5/339 and Silsilatul-Ahādith As-Sahīhah 2/697 (no. 972).

yuhyee wa yumeetu wa Huwa 'alaa kulli shay'in Qadeer.

None has the right to be worshipped but Allāh alone, Who has no partner. His is the dominion and His is the praise. He brings life and He causes death, and He is Able to do all things. (Recite ten times in Arabic after the *Maghrib* and *Fajr* prayers.)[1]

٧٣- «اللّٰهُمَّ إِنِّي أَسْأَلُكَ عِلْمًا نَافِعًا، وَرِزْقًا طَيِّبًا، وَعَمَلًا مُتَقَبَّلًا».

73. *Allaahumma 'innee 'as'aluka 'ilman naafi'an, wa rizqan tayyiban, wa 'amalan mutaqabbalan.*

O Allāh, I ask You for knowledge that is of benefit, a good provision, and deeds that will be accepted. (Recite in Arabic after the *Fajr* prayer.)[2]

---

[1] At-Tirmithi 5/515, Ahmad 4/227. See its checking in Ibn Al-Qayyim Al-Jawziyyah's *Zādul-Ma'ād* 1/300.

[2] Ibn Mājah and others. See Al-Albāni, *Sahih Ibn Mājah* 1/152 and *Majma'uz-Zawā'id* 10/111.

26. *Istikhārah* (seeking Allāh's Counsel)

Jābir bin Abdullah ﷺ said: The Prophet
ﷺ used to teach us to seek Allāh's
Counsel in all matters, as he used to teach
us a *Surah* from the Qur'ān. He would
say: When anyone of you has an
important matter to decide, let him pray
two *Rak'ahs* other than the obligatory
prayer, and then say:

٧٤-«اللّهُمَّ إِنِّي أَسْتَخِيرُكَ بِعِلْمِكَ، وَأَسْتَقْدِرُكَ
بِقُدْرَتِكَ، وَأَسْأَلُكَ مِنْ فَضْلِكَ الْعَظِيمِ، فَإِنَّكَ
تَقْدِرُ وَلَا أَقْدِرُ، وَتَعْلَمُ، وَلَا أَعْلَمُ، وَأَنْتَ
عَلَّامُ الْغُيُوبِ، اللّهُمَّ إِنْ كُنْتَ تَعْلَمُ أَنَّ هَذَا
الْأَمْرَ- خَيْرٌ لِي فِي دِينِي وَمَعَاشِي وَعَاقِبَةِ
أَمْرِي- عَاجِلِهِ وَآجِلِهِ- فَاقْدُرْهُ لِي وَيَسِّرْهُ لِي
ثُمَّ بَارِكْ لِي فِيهِ، وَإِنْ كُنْتَ تَعْلَمُ أَنَّ هَذَا الْأَمْرَ
شَرٌّ لِي فِي دِينِي وَمَعَاشِي وَعَاقِبَةِ أَمْرِي –
عَاجِلِهِ وَآجِلِهِ- فَاصْرِفْهُ عَنِّي وَاصْرِفْنِي عَنْهُ

وَاقْدُرْ لِيَ الْخَيْرَ حَيْثُ كَانَ ثُمَّ أَرْضِنِي بِهِ».

74. Allaahumma 'innee 'astakheeruka
bi'ilmika, wa 'astaqdiruka biqudratika, wa
'as'aluka min fadhlikal-'Adheemi, fa'innaka
taqdiru wa laa 'aqdiru, wa ta'lamu, wa laa
'a'lamu, wa 'Anta 'Allaamul-Ghuyoobi,
Allaahumma 'in kunta ta'lamu 'anna haathal-
'amra – [then mention the thing to be
decided] Khayrun lee fee deenee wa
ma'aashee wa 'aaqibati 'amree – [or say]
'Aajilihi wa 'aajilihi – Faqdurhu lee wa
yassirhu lee thumma baarik lee feehi, wa 'in
kunta ta'lamu 'anna haathal-'amra sharrun
lee fee deenee wa ma'aashee wa 'aaqibati
'amree – [or say] 'Aajilihi wa 'aajilihi –
Fasrifhu 'annee wasrifnee 'anhu waqdur liyal-
khayra haythu kaana thumma 'ardhinee bihi.

O Allāh, I seek the counsel of Your
Knowledge, and I seek the help of Your
Omnipotence, and I beseech You for Your
Magnificent Grace. Surely, You are
Capable and I am not. You know and I
know not, and You are the Knower of the

unseen. O Allāh, if You know that this matter [then mention the thing to be decided] is good for me in my religion and in my life and for my welfare in the life to come, – [or say: in this life and the afterlife] – then ordain it for me and make it easy for me, then bless me in it. And if You know that this matter is bad for me in my religion and in my life and for my welfare in the life to come, – [or say: in this life and the afterlife] – then distance it from me, and distance me from it, and ordain for me what is good wherever it may be, and help me to be content with it.[1]

Whoever seeks the counsel of the Creator will not regret it and whoever seeks the advice of the believers will feel confident about his decisions. Allāh said in the Qur'ān:

$$﴿وَشَاوِرْهُمْ فِي ٱلْأَمْرِ فَإِذَا عَزَمْتَ فَتَوَكَّلْ عَلَى ٱللَّهِ﴾$$

"And consult them in the affair. Then when you have taken a decision, put your

[1] Al-Bukhāri 7/162.

trust in Allāh.''[1]

27. Words of remembrance for morning and evening

All praise is due to Allāh alone, and peace and blessings be upon him after whom there is no other Prophet.[2]

٧٥-أَعُوذُ بِاللهِ مِنَ الشَّيْطَانِ الرَّجِيمِ ﴿ٱللَّهُ لَآ
إِلَهَ إِلَّا هُوَ ٱلْحَيُّ ٱلْقَيُّومُ لَا تَأْخُذُهُ سِنَةٌ وَلَا نَوْمٌ
لَّهُ مَا فِى ٱلسَّمَوَاتِ وَمَا فِى ٱلْأَرْضِ مَن ذَا ٱلَّذِى يَشْفَعُ

---

[1] Aal-'Imrān 3:159.

[2] Anas ؓ said that he heard the Prophet ﷺ say: "That I sit with people remembering Almighty Allāh from the morning (Fajr) prayer until sunrise is more beloved to me than freeing four slaves from among the Children of Isma'il. That I sit with people remembering Allāh from the afternoon ('Asr) prayer until the sun sets is more beloved to me than freeing four slaves from among the Children of Isma'il.'' This was reported by Abu Dawud (no. 3667). Al-Albāni graded it good in Sahih Abu Dawud 2/698.

عِنْدَهُ إِلَّا بِإِذْنِهِ يَعْلَمُ مَا بَيْنَ أَيْدِيهِمْ وَمَا خَلْفَهُمْ وَلَا يُحِيطُونَ بِشَيْءٍ مِّنْ عِلْمِهِ إِلَّا بِمَا شَاءَ وَسِعَ كُرْسِيُّهُ السَّمَوَاتِ وَالْأَرْضَ وَلَا يَؤُودُهُ حِفْظُهُمَا وَهُوَ الْعَلِيُّ الْعَظِيمُ ۞

75. 'A'oot<u>h</u>u billaahi minash-Shaytaanir-rajeem. Allaahu laa 'ilaaha 'illaa Huwal-Hayyul-Qayyoom, laa ta'khu<u>th</u>uhu sinatun wa laa nawm, lahu maa fis-samaawaati wa maa fil-'ardh, man <u>th</u>al-la<u>th</u>ee yashfa'u 'indahu 'illaa bi'i<u>th</u>nih, ya'lamu maa bayna 'aydeehim wa maa khalfahum, wa laa yuheetoona bishay'im-min 'ilmihi 'illaa bimaa shaa'a, wasi'a kursiyyuhus samaawaati wal'ardh, wa laa ya'ooduhu hif<u>dh</u>uhumaa, wa Huwal-'Aliyyul-'A<u>dh</u>eem.

I seek refuge in Allāh from Satan the outcast. – Allāh! There is none worthy of worship but He, the Ever Living, the One Who sustains and protects all that exists. Neither slumber nor sleep overtakes Him. To Him belongs whatever is in the heavens and whatever is on the earth. Who is he that can intercede with Him except with His Permission? He knows what happens to them in this world, and what will happen to them in the Hereafter. And they will never encompass anything of His Knowledge except that which He wills. His Throne extends over the heavens and the earth, and He feels no fatigue in guarding and preserving them. And He is the Most High, the Most Great.[1]

٧٦- بِسْمِ اللَّهِ الرَّحْمَنِ الرَّحِيمِ ﴿قُلْ هُوَ

---

[1] Whoever says this when he rises in the morning will be protected from jinns until he retires in the evening, and whoever says it when retiring in the evening will be protected from them until he rises in the morning. It was reported by Al-Hākim 1/562, Al-Albāni graded it as authentic in *Sahīhut-Targhīb wat-Tarhīb* 1/273, and traces it to An-Nasā'i and At-Tabarāni. He says that At-Tabarāni's chain of transmission is reliable (*Jayyid*).

اللّٰهُ أَحَدٌ ٥ اللّٰهُ الصَّمَدُ ٥ لَمْ يَلِدْ وَلَمْ يُولَدْ ٥ وَلَمْ يَكُن لَّهُ كُفُوًا أَحَدٌ ٥

76. Bismillaahir-Rahmaanir-Raheem. *Qul Huwallaahu 'Ahad. Allaahus-Samad. Lam yalid wa lam yoolad. Wa lam yakun lahu kufuwan 'ahad.*

With the Name of Allāh, the Most Gracious, the Most Merciful. Say: He is Allāh (the) One. The Self-Sufficient Master, Whom all creatures need, He begets not nor was He begotten, and there is none equal to Him.

بِسْمِ اللّٰهِ الرَّحْمٰنِ الرَّحِيمِ ﴿قُلْ أَعُوذُ بِرَبِّ الْفَلَقِ ٥ مِن شَرِّ مَا خَلَقَ ٥ وَمِن شَرِّ غَاسِقٍ إِذَا وَقَبَ ٥ وَمِن شَرِّ النَّفَّاثَاتِ فِي الْعُقَدِ ٥ وَمِن شَرِّ حَاسِدٍ إِذَا حَسَدَ ﴾

Bismillaahir-Rahmaanir-Raheem. Qul 'a'oothu birabbil-falaq. Min sharri ma khalaq. Wa min sharri ghaasiqin 'ithaa waqab. Wa min sharrin-naffaathaati fil-'uqad. Wa min sharri haasidin 'iṯẖaa hasad.

With the Name of Allāh, the Most Gracious, the Most Merciful. Say: I seek refuge with (Allāh) the Lord of the daybreak, from the evil of what He has created, and from the evil of the darkening (night) as it comes with its darkness, and from the evil of those who practice witchcraft when they blow in the knots, and from the evil of the envier when he envies.

بِسْمِ اللَّهِ الرَّحْمَٰنِ الرَّحِيمِ ﴿قُلْ أَعُوذُ بِرَبِّ النَّاسِ ○ مَلِكِ النَّاسِ ○ إِلَٰهِ النَّاسِ ○ مِن شَرِّ الْوَسْوَاسِ الْخَنَّاسِ ○ الَّذِي يُوَسْوِسُ فِي صُدُورِ النَّاسِ ○ مِنَ الْجِنَّةِ وَالنَّاسِ ﴾ .

Bismillaahir-Rahmaanir-Raheem. Qul 'a'ooṯẖu birabbin-naas. Malikin-naas. 'Ilaahin-naas. Min sharril-waswaasil-khannaas. Allaṯẖee yuwaswisu fee sudoorin-naas. Minal-jinnati wannaas.

With the Name of Allāh, the Most Gracious, the Most Merciful. Say: I seek refuge with (Allāh) the Lord of mankind, the King of mankind, the God of mankind, from the evil of the whisperer who withdraws, Who whispers in the breasts of mankind, of jinns and men.

(Recite these three times each in Arabic.)[1]

٧٧-«أَصْبَحْنَا وَأَصْبَحَ الْمُلْكُ لِلَّهِ وَالْحَمْدُ لِلَّهِ، لَا إِلَهَ إِلَّا اللهُ وَحْدَهُ لَا شَرِيكَ لَهُ، لَهُ الْمُلْكُ وَلَهُ الْحَمْدُ وَهُوَ عَلَى كُلِّ شَيْءٍ قَدِيرٌ، رَبِّ أَسْأَلُكَ خَيْرَ مَا فِي هَذَا الْيَوْمِ وَخَيْرَ مَا بَعْدَهُ، وَأَعُوذُ بِكَ مِنْ شَرِّ مَا فِي هَذَا الْيَوْمِ وَشَرِّ مَا بَعْدَهُ، رَبِّ أَعُوذُ بِكَ مِنَ الْكَسَلِ، وَسُوءِ الْكِبَرِ، رَبِّ أَعُوذُ بِكَ مِنْ عَذَابٍ فِي النَّارِ وَعَذَابٍ فِي الْقَبْرِ».

---

[1] Whoever recites these three times in the morning and in the evening, they will suffice him (as a protection) against everything. The *Hadith* was reported by Abu Dawud 4/322, and At-Tirmithi 5/567. See Al-Albāni's *Sahih At-Tirmithi* 3/182.

77. 'Asbahnaa wa 'asbahal-mulku lillaahi walhamdu lillaahi, laa 'ilaaha 'illallaahu wahdahu laa shareeka lahu, lahul-mulku wa lahul-hamdu wa Huwa 'alaa kulli shay'in Qadeer. Rabbi 'as'aluka khayra maa fee haathal-yawmi wa khayra maa ba'dahu wa 'a'oothu bika min sharri maa fee haathal-yawmi wa sharri maa ba'dahu, Rabbi 'a'oothu bika minal-kasali, wa soo'il-kibari, Rabbi 'a'oothu bika min 'athaabin fin-naari wa 'athaabin fil-qabri.

We have entered a new day[1] and with it all dominion is Allāh's. Praise is to Allāh. None has the right to be worshipped but Allāh alone, Who has no partner. To Allāh belongs the dominion, and to Him is the praise and He is Able to do all things. My Lord, I ask You for the goodness of this day and of the days that come after it, and I seek refuge in You

---

[1] When you say this in the evening you should say 'Amsaynaa wa'amsal-mulku lillaah: "We have ended another day and with it all dominion is Allāh's."

from the evil of this day and of the days that come after it.[1] My Lord, I seek refuge in You from laziness and helpless old age. My Lord, I seek refuge in You from the punishment of Hell-fire, and from the punishment of the grave.[2]

٧٨-«اللَّهُمَّ بِكَ أَصْبَحْنَا، وَبِكَ أَمْسَيْنَا، وَبِكَ نَحْيَا، وَبِكَ نَمُوتُ وَإِلَيْكَ النُّشُورُ».

78. Allaahumma bika 'asbahnaa, wa bika 'amsaynaa, wa bika nahyaa, wa bika namootu wa 'ilaykan-nushoor.

O Allāh, by You we enter the morning and by You we enter the evening,[3] by

---

[1] When you say this in the evening you should say: Rabbi 'as'aluka khayra maa fee haathihil-laylati, wa khayra maa ba'dahaa, wa 'a'oothu bika min sharri maa fee haathihil-laylati wa sharri maa ba'dahaa: "I ask You for the good things of this night and of the nights that come after it and I seek refuge in You from the evil of this night and of the nights that come after it."

[2] Muslim 4/2088.

[3] When you say this in the evening you

98

You we live and and by You we die, and
to You is the Final Return.[1]

٧٩-«اللَّهُمَّ أَنْتَ رَبِّي لَا إِلَهَ إِلَّا أَنْتَ، خَلَقْتَنِي
وَأَنَا عَبْدُكَ، وَأَنَا عَلَى عَهْدِكَ وَوَعْدِكَ مَا
اسْتَطَعْتُ، أَعُوذُ بِكَ مِنْ شَرِّ مَا صَنَعْتُ، أَبُوءُ
لَكَ بِنِعْمَتِكَ عَلَيَّ، وَأَبُوءُ بِذَنْبِي فَاغْفِرْ لِي فَإِنَّهُ
لَا يَغْفِرُ الذُّنُوبَ إِلَّا أَنْتَ».

79. *Allaahumma 'Anta Rabbee laa 'ilaaha
'illaa 'Anta, khalaqtanee wa 'anaa 'abduka, wa
'anaa 'alaa 'ahdika wa wa'dika mas-tata'tu,
'a'oothu bika min sharri maa sana'tu, 'aboo'u
laka bini'matika 'alayya, wa 'aboo'u bithanbee
faghfir lee fa'innahu laa yaghfiruth-thunooba
'illaa 'Anta.*

---

should say: *Allaahumma bika 'amsaynaa wa bika
'asbahnaa, wa bika nahyaa, wa bika namoot, wa
'ilaykal-maseer:* "O Allāh, You bring us the end
of the day as You bring us its beginning, You
bring us life and you bring us death, and to
You is our fate."

[1] *Sahih At-Tirmithi* 3/142.

O Allāh, You are my Lord, there is none worthy of worship but You. You created me and I am your slave. I keep Your covenant, and my pledge to You so far as I am able. I seek refuge in You from the evil of what I have done. I admit to Your blessings upon me, and I admit to my misdeeds. Forgive me, for there is none who may forgive sins but You.[1]

٨٠- «اللَّهُمَّ إِنِّي أَصْبَحْتُ أُشْهِدُكَ وَأُشْهِدُ حَمَلَةَ عَرْشِكَ، وَمَلاَئِكَتَكَ وَجَمِيعَ خَلْقِكَ، أَنَّكَ أَنْتَ اللهُ لَا إِلَهَ إِلَّا أَنْتَ وَحْدَكَ لَا شَرِيكَ لَكَ، وَأَنَّ مُحَمَّدًا عَبْدُكَ وَرَسُولُكَ».

80. *Allaahumma 'innee 'asbahtu 'ush-hiduka wa 'ush-hidu hamalata 'arshika, wa*

---

[1] Whoever recites this with conviction in the evening and dies during that night shall enter Paradise, and whoever recites it with conviction in the morning and dies during that day shall enter Paradise, Al-Bukhāri 7/150. Other reports are in An-Nasā'i and At-Tirmithi.

malaa'ikataka wa jamee'a khalqika, 'annaka 'Antallaahu laa 'ilaaha 'illaa 'Anta wahdaka laa shareeka laka, wa 'anna Muhammadan 'abduka wa Rasooluka.

O Allāh, I have entered a new morning[1] and call upon You and upon the bearers of Your Throne, upon Your angels and all creation to bear witness that surely You are Allāh, there is none worthy of worship but You alone, You have no partners, and that Muhammad is Your slave and Your Messenger. (Recite four times in Arabic.)[2]

٨١ - «اللَّهُمَّ مَا أَصْبَحَ بِي مِنْ نِعْمَةٍ أَوْ بِأَحَدٍ مِنْ

---

[1] When you say this in the evening you should say, *Allaahumma 'innee 'amsaytu....*: "O Allāh, I have ended another day..."

[2] "Allāh will spare whoever says this four times in the morning or evening from the fire of Hell," Abu Dawud 4/317. It was also reported by Al-Bukhāri in *Al-'Adab Al-Mufrad*, An-Nasā'i in *'Amalul-Yawm wal-Laylah* and Ibn As-Sunni. Nasā'i's and Abu Dawud's chains of transmission are good (*Hasan*), Ibn Bāz, p. 23.

خَلْقِكَ فَمِنْكَ وَحْدَكَ لَا شَرِيكَ لَكَ، فَلَكَ الْحَمْدُ وَلَكَ الشُّكْرُ».

81. *Allaahumma maa 'asbaha bee min ni'matin 'aw bi'ahadin min khalqika faminka wahdaka laa shareeka laka, falakal-hamdu wa lakash-shukru.*

O Allāh, whatever blessing has been received by me or anyone of Your creation[1] is from You alone, You have no partner. All praise is for you and thanks is to You.[2]

---

[1] When you say this in the evening, you should say: *Allaahumma maa 'amsaa bee...*: "O Allāh, as I... enter this evening..."

[2] Whoever recites this in the morning, has completed his obligation to thank Allāh for that day; and whoever says it in the evening, has completed his obligation for that night. Abu Dawud 4/318, An-Nasā'i *'Amalul-Yawm wal-Laylah* (no. 7), Ibn As-Sunni (no. 41), Ibn Hibban (no. 2361). Its chain of transmission is good (*Hasan*), Ibn Bāz, p. 24.

٨٢-«اللَّهُمَّ عَافِنِي فِي بَدَنِي، اللَّهُمَّ عَافِنِي فِي سَمْعِي، اللَّهُمَّ عَافِنِي فِي بَصَرِي، لَا إِلَهَ إِلَّا أَنْتَ. اللَّهُمَّ إِنِّي أَعُوذُ بِكَ مِنَ الْكُفْرِ وَالْفَقْرِ، وَ أَعُوذُ بِكَ مِنْ عَذَابِ الْقَبْرِ، لَا إِلَهَ إِلَّا أَنْتَ».

82. *Allaahumma 'aafinee fee badanee, Allaahumma 'aafinee fee sam'ee, Allaahumma 'aafinee fee basaree, laa 'ilaaha 'illaa 'Anta. Allaahumma 'innee 'a'oothu bika minal-kufri, walfaqri, wa 'a'oothu bika min 'athaabil-qabri, laa 'ilaaha 'illaa 'Anta.*

O Allāh, make me healthy in my body. O Allāh, preserve for me my hearing. O Allāh, preserve for me my sight. There is none worthy of worship but You. O Allāh, I seek refuge in You from disbelief and poverty and I seek refuge in You from the punishment of the grave. There is none worthy of worship but You. (Recite three times in Arabic.)[1]

---

[1] Abu Dawud 4/324, Ahmad 5/42, An-Nasā'i, *'Amalul-Yawm wal-Laylah* (no. 22), Ibn

٨٣ - ﴿حَسْبِيَ ٱللَّهُ لَا إِلَٰهَ إِلَّا هُوَ عَلَيْهِ تَوَكَّلْتُ وَهُوَ رَبُّ ٱلْعَرْشِ ٱلْعَظِيمِ﴾

83. Hasbiyallaahu laa 'ilaaha 'illaa Huwa 'alayhi tawakkaltu wa Huwa Rabbul-'Arshil-'Adheem.

Allāh is sufficient for me. There is none worthy of worship but Him. I have placed my trust in Him, He is Lord of the Majestic Throne. (Recite seven times in Arabic.)[1]

٨٤ - «اللَّهُمَّ إِنِّي أَسْأَلُكَ ٱلْعَفْوَ وَٱلْعَافِيَةَ فِي

As- Sunni (no. 69), Al-Bukhāri Al-'Adab Al-Mufrad. Its chain of transmission is good (Hasan), Ibn Bāz, p. 26.
[1] Allāh will grant whoever recites this seven times in the morning or evening whatever he desires from this world or the next, Ibn As-Sunni (no. 71), Abu Dawud 4/321. Both reports are attributed directly to the Prophet ﷺ (Marfu'). The chain of transmission is sound (Sahīh). Ibn As-Sunni.

الدُّنْيَا وَالْآخِرَةِ، اللَّهُمَّ إِنِّي أَسْأَلُكَ الْعَفْوَ وَالْعَافِيَةَ فِي دِينِي وَدُنْيَايَ وَأَهْلِي، وَمَالِي، اللَّهُمَّ اسْتُرْ عَوْرَاتِي، وَآمِنْ رَوْعَاتِي، اللَّهُمَّ احْفَظْنِي مِنْ بَيْنِ يَدَيَّ، وَمِنْ خَلْفِي، وَعَنْ يَمِينِي، وَعَنْ شِمَالِي، وَمِنْ فَوْقِي، وَأَعُوذُ بِعَظَمَتِكَ أَنْ أُغْتَالَ مِنْ تَحْتِي».

84. *Allaahumma 'innee 'as'alukal-'afwa wal'aafiyata fid-dunyaa wal'aakhirati, Allaahumma 'innee 'as'alukal-'afwa wal'aafiyata fee deenee wa dunyaaya wa 'ahlee, wa maalee, Allaahum-mastur 'awraatee, wa 'aamin raw'aatee, Allaahum-mahfadhnee min bayni yadayya, wa min khalfee, wa 'an yameenee, wa 'an shimaalee, wa min fawqee, wa 'a'oothu bi'adhamatika 'an 'ughtaala min tahtee.*

O Allāh, I seek Your forgiveness and Your protection in this world and the next. O Allāh, I seek Your forgiveness and Your protection in my religion, in my worldly affairs, in my family and in my wealth. O Allāh, conceal my secrets and preserve me from anguish. O Allāh, guard me from what is in front of me and behind me, from my left, and from my right, and from above me. I seek refuge in Your Greatness from being struck down from beneath me.[1]

٨٥- «اللَّهُمَّ عَالِمَ الْغَيْبِ وَالشَّهَادَةِ فَاطِرَ السَّمَوَاتِ وَالْأَرْضِ، رَبَّ كُلِّ شَيْءٍ وَمَلِيكَهُ، أَشْهَدُ أَنْ لَا إِلَهَ إِلَّا أَنْتَ، أَعُوذُ بِكَ مِنْ شَرِّ نَفْسِي، وَمِنْ شَرِّ الشَّيْطَانِ وَشِرْكِهِ، وَأَنْ أَقْتَرِفَ عَلَى نَفْسِي سُوءًا، أَوْ أَجُرَّهُ إِلَى مُسْلِمٍ».

85. *Allāahumma 'Aalimal-ghaybi wash-shahaadati faatiras-samaawaati wal'ardhi, Rabba kulli shay'in wa maleekahu, 'ash-hadu 'an laa 'ilaaha 'illaa 'Anta, 'aoothu bika min sharri nafsee, wa min sharrish-shaytaani wa shirkihi, wa 'an 'aqtarifa 'alaa nafsee soo'an,*

---

[1] *Sahih Ibn Mājah* 2/332 and Abu Dawud.

'aw 'ajurrahu 'ilaa Muslimin.

O Allāh, Knower of the unseen and the evident, Maker of the heavens and the earth, Lord of everything and its Possessor, I bear witness that there is none worthy of worship but You. I seek refuge in You from the evil of my soul and from the evil of Satan and his helpers. (I seek refuge in You) from bringing evil upon my soul and from harming any Muslim.[1]

٨٦-«بِسْمِ اللهِ الَّذِي لَا يَضُرُّ مَعَ اسْمِهِ شَيْءٌ فِي الْأَرْضِ وَلَا فِي السَّمَاءِ وَهُوَ السَّمِيعُ الْعَلِيمُ» .

86. *Bismillaahil-lathee laa yadhurru ma'as-mihi shay'un fil-'ardhi wa laa fis-samaa'i wa Huwas-Samee'ul-'Aleem.*

In the Name of Allāh, Who with His Name nothing can cause harm in the earth nor in the heavens, and He is the

---

[1] *Sahih At-Tirmithi* 3/142 and Abu Dawud.

All-Hearing, the All-Knowing. (Recite three times in Arabic.)[1]

٨٧- «رَضِيتُ بِاللهِ رَبًّا، وَبِالإِسْلَامِ دِينًا،
وَبِمُحَمَّدٍ ﷺ نَبِيًّا».

87. Radheetu billaahi Rabban, wa bil-'Islaami deenan, wa bi-Muhammadin (sallallaahu 'alayhi wa sallama) Nabiyyan.

I am pleased with Allāh as my Lord, with Islam as my religion and with Muhammad (peace and blessings of Allāh be upon him) as my Prophet. (Recite three times in Arabic.)[2]

---

[1] "Whoever recites it three times in the morning will not be afflicted by any calamity before evening, and whoever recites it three times in the evening will not be overtaken by any calamity before morning." Abu Dawud 4/323, At-Tirmithi 5/465, Ibn Mājah 2/332, Ahmad. Ibn Mājah's chain of transmission is good (Hasan), Ibn Bāz, p. 39.

[2] "Allāh has promised that anyone who says this three times every morning or evening will be pleased on the Day of Resurrection."

٨٨- «يَا حَيُّ يَا قَيُّومُ بِرَحْمَتِكَ أَسْتَغِيثُ أَصْلِحْ
لِي شَأْنِي كُلَّهُ وَلَا تَكِلْنِي إِلَى نَفْسِي طَرْفَةَ
عَيْنٍ».

88. Yaa Hayyu yaa Qayyoomu birahmatika
'astagheethu 'aslih lee sha'nee kullahu wa laa
takilnee 'ilaa nafsee tarfata 'aynin.

O Ever Living One, O Eternal One, by
Your mercy I call on You to set right all
my affairs. Do not place me in charge of
my soul even for the blinking of an eye
(i.e. a moment).[1]

٨٩- «أَصْبَحْنَا وَأَصْبَحَ الْمُلْكُ لله رَبِّ
الْعَالَمِينَ، اللَّهُمَّ إِنِّي أَسْأَلُكَ خَيْرَ هَذَا الْيَوْمِ:

Ahmad 4/337, An-Nasā'i, 'Amalul-Yawm wal-
Laylah p. 4, Ibn As-Sunni (no. 68), At-Tirmithi
5/465. Its chain of transmission is good
(Hasan), Ibn Bāz, p. 39.
[1] Its chain of transmission is sound (Sahīh),
Al-Hākim 1/545, see Albāni, Sahihut-Targhib
wat-Tarhib,1/273.

فَتْحَهُ، وَنَصْرَهُ وَنُورَهُ، وَبَرَكَتَهُ، وَهُدَاهُ، وَأَعُوذُ
بِكَ مِنْ شَرِّ مَا فِيهِ وَشَرِّ مَا بَعْدَهُ».

89. 'Asbahnaa wa 'asbahal-mulku lillaahi Rabbil-'aalameen, Allaahumma 'innee 'as'aluka khayra haa<u>th</u>al-yawmi: Fathahu wa nasrahu wa noorahu, wa barakatahu, wa hudaahu, wa'a'oo<u>th</u>u bika min sharri maa feehi wa sharri maa ba'dahu.

We have entered a new day and with it all the dominion which belongs to Allāh, Lord of all that exists. O Allāh, I ask You for the goodness of this day,[1] its victory, its help, its light, its blessings, and its guidance. I seek refuge in You from the evil that is in it and from the evil that follows it.[2]

---

[1] For evening recitation, say here: Allaahumma 'innee 'as'aluka khayra haa<u>th</u>ihil-laylati: "My Lord, I ask You for the good things of this night."

[2] Abu Dawud 4/322. Its transmission chain is good (Hasan). See also Ibn Al-Qayyim, Zādul-Ma'ād 2/273.

٩٠- «أَصْبَحْنَا عَلَى فِطْرَةِ الْإِسْلَامِ وَعَلَى كَلِمَةِ
الْإِخْلَاصِ، وَعَلَى دِينِ نَبِيِّنَا مُحَمَّدٍ ﷺ،
وَعَلَى مِلَّةِ أَبِينَا إِبْرَاهِيمَ، حَنِيفًا مُسْلِمًا وَمَا
كَانَ مِنَ الْمُشْرِكِينَ».

90. 'Asbahnaa 'alaa fitratil-'Islaami wa 'alaa
kalimatil-'ikhlaasi, wa 'alaa deeni Nabiyyinaa
Muhammadin (sallallaahu 'alayhi wa
sallama), wa 'alaa millati 'abeenaa
'Ibraaheema, haneefan Musliman wa maa
kaana minal-mushrikeen.

We have entered a new day[1] upon the
natural religion of Islam, the word of
sincere devotion, the religion of our
Prophet Muhammad (peace and blessings
of Allāh be upon him), and the faith of
our father Ibrahim. He was upright (in
worshipping Allah), and a Muslim. He
was not of those who worship others

---

[1] When you say this in the evening, you
should say: 'Amsaynaa 'alaa fitratil-'Islaam...:
"We end this day..."

111

besides Allāh.[1]

٩١ - «سُبْحَانَ اللهِ وَبِحَمْدِهِ» .

91. *Subhaanallaahi wa bihamdihi.*

Glory is to Allāh and praise is to Him.
(Recite one hundred times in Arabic.)[2]

٩٢ - «لَا إِلَهَ إِلَّا اللهُ وَحْدَهُ لَا شَرِيكَ لَهُ، لَهُ
الْمُلْكُ وَلَهُ الْحَمْدُ وَهُوَ عَلَى كُلِّ شَيْءٍ قَدِيرٌ» .

92. *Laa 'ilaaha 'illallaahu wahdahu laa
shareeka lahu, lahul-mulku wa lahul-hamdu,
wa Huwa 'alaa kulli shay'in Qadeer.*

None has the right to be worshipped but
Allāh alone, Who has no partner. His is
the dominion and His is the praise and

---

[1] Ahmad 3/406-7, 5/123, An-Nasā'i, *'Amalul-Yawm wal-Laylah* (no. 34), At-Tirmiṭhi 4/209.
[2] "Whoever recites this one hundred times in the morning and in the evening will not be surpassed on the Day of Resurrection by anyone having done better than this except for someone who had recited it more." Al-Bukhāri 4/2071.

He is Able to do all things. (Recite ten times[1] in Arabic or one time to ward off laziness.)[2]

---

[1] Allāh will write ten *Hasanaat* (rewards) for whoever recites this ten times in the morning, and forgive him ten misdeeds and give him the reward of freeing ten slaves and protect him from Satan. Whoever recites this ten times in the evening will get this same reward. An-Nasā'i, '*Amalul-Yawm wal-Laylah* (no. 24). Its chain of transmission is sound (*Sahīh*). Albāni 1/272. Abu Hurayrah ﷺ narrated that the Prophet ﷺ said: "Allāh will write one hundred *Hasanat* for whoever says 'There is no God but Allāh alone, He has no partner. To Allāh is possession of everything, and to Him all praise is. He is Capable of all things' ten times in the morning, and forgive him one hundred misdeeds. He will have the reward of freeing a slave and will be protected from Satan throughout the day unto dusk. Whoever says it in the evening will have the same reward." Ahmad 8/704, 16/293. Its chain of transmission is good (*Hasan*), Ibn Bāz, p. 44.

[2] Whoever recites this in the morning, will

٩٣-«لَا إِلَهَ إِلَّا اللهُ وَحْدَهُ لَا شَرِيكَ لَهُ، لَهُ الْمُلْكُ وَلَهُ الْحَمْدُ وَهُوَ عَلَى كُلِّ شَيْءٍ قَدِيرٌ».

93. *Laa 'ilaaha 'illallaahu wahdahu laa shareeka lahu, lahul-mulku wa lahul-hamdu wa Huwa 'alaa kulli shay'in Qadeer.*

None has the right to be worshipped but Allāh alone, Who has no partner. His is the dominion and His is the praise and He is Able to do all things. (Recite one hundred times in Arabic upon rising in the morning.)[1]

---

have the reward of freeing a slave from the Children of Isma'il. Ten *Hasanaat* (rewards) will be written for him, and he will be forgiven ten misdeeds, raised up ten degrees, and be protected from Satan until evening. Whoever says it in the evening will have the same reward until morning. Abu Dawud 4/319, 3/957, Ahmad 4/60, Ibn Mājah 2/331, Ibn Al-Qayyim *Zādul-Ma'ād* 2/388. Its chain of transmission is sound (*Sahih*). Al-Albāni 1/270.
[1] Whoever recites this one hundred times a day will have the reward of freeing ten slaves.

٩٤ –«سُبْحَانَ اللهِ وَبِحَمْدِهِ: عَدَدَ خَلْقِهِ، وَرِضَا
نَفْسِهِ، وَزِنَةَ عَرْشِهِ وَمِدَادَ كَلِمَاتِهِ».

94. *Subhaanallaahi wa bihamdihi: 'Adada
khalqihi, wa ridhaa nafsihi, wa zinata 'arshihi
wa midaada kalimaatihi.*

Glory is to Allāh and praise is to Him, by
the multitude of His creation, by His
Pleasure, by the weight of His Throne,
and by the extent of His Words. (Recite
three times in Arabic upon rising in the
morning.)[1]

٩٥ –«اللَّهُمَّ إِنِّي أَسْأَلُكَ عِلْمًا نَافِعًا، وَرِزْقًا
طَيِّبًا، وَعَمَلًا مُتَقَبَّلًا».

One hundred *Hasanaat* (rewards) will be
written for him and one hundred misdeeds
will be washed away. He will be shielded from
Satan until the evening. No one will be able to
present anything better than this except for
someone who has recited more than this. Al-
Bukhāri 4/95, Muslim 4/2071.

[1] Muslim 4/2090.

95. *Allaahumma 'innee 'as'aluka 'ilman naafi'an, wa rizqan tayyiban, wa 'amalan mutaqabbalan.*

O Allāh, I ask You for knowledge that is of benefit, a good provision, and deeds that will be accepted. (Recite in Arabic upon rising in the morning.)[1]

٩٦-«أَسْتَغْفِرُ اللهَ وَأَتُوبُ إِلَيْهِ» .

96. *'Astaghfirullaaha wa 'atoobu 'ilayhi.*

I seek the forgiveness of Allāh and repent to Him. (Recite one hundred times in Arabic during the day.)[2]

٩٧-«أَعُوذُ بِكَلِمَاتِ اللهِ التَّامَّاتِ مِنْ شَرِّ مَا خَلَقَ» .

97. *'A'oothu bikalimaatil-laahit-taammaati min sharri maa khalaqa.*

---

[1] Ibn As-Sunni, no. 54, Ibn Mājah no. 925. Its chain of transmission is good (*Hasan*), Ibn Al-Qayyim 2/375.
[2] Al-Bukhāri, cf. Al-Asqalāni, *Fathul-Bāri* 11/101, Muslim 4/2075.

I seek refuge in the Perfect Words of Allāh from the evil of what He has created. (Recite three times in Arabic in the evening.)[1]

٩٨- «اللَّهُمَّ صَلِّ وَسَلِّمْ عَلَى نَبِيِّنَا مُحَمَّدٍ».

98. *Allaahumma salli wa sallim 'alaa Nabiyyinaa Muhammadin.*

O Allāh, we ask for your peace and blessings upon our Prophet Muhammad. (Recite ten times in Arabic.)[2]

---

[1] Whoever recites this three times in the evening will be protected from insect stings, Ahmad 2/290, An-Nasā'i, *'Amalul-Yawm wal-Laylah* no. 590, At-Tirmithi 3/187, Ibn As-Sunni no. 68. According to Al-Albāni, Ibn Mājah's (2/266) chain of transmission is sound (*Sahih*), and following Ibn Bāz 45, At-Tirmithi's report is good (*Hasan*).

[2] The Prophet ﷺ said: "Who recites blessings upon me ten times in the morning and ten times in the evening will obtain my intercession on the Day of Resurrection." At-Tabarāni reported this *Hadith* together with two chains of transmission. One of them is

28. What to say before sleeping

(Cup your palms together, blow gently into them and then recite:)

99. *Bismillaahir-Rahmaanir-Raheem. Qul Huwallaahu 'Ahad. Allaahus-Samad. Lam yalid wa lam yoolad. Wa lam yakun lahu kufuwan 'ahad.*

With the Name of Allāh, the Most Gracious, the Most Merciful. Say: He is Allāh (the) One. The Self-Sufficient Master, Whom all creatures need, He begets not nor was He begotten, and none is equal to Him.

---

reliable (*Jayyid*). See Haythami's *Majma'uz-Zawā'id* 10/120, and Al-Albāni's *Sahīhut-Targhīb wat-Tarhīb* 1/273.

الفَلَقِ ٥ مِن شَرِّ مَا خَلَقَ ٥ وَمِن شَرِّ غَاسِقٍ إِذَا وَقَبَ ٥ وَمِن شَرِّ النَّفَّاثَٰتِ فِى ٱلْعُقَدِ ٥وَمِن شَرِّ حَاسِدٍ إِذَا حَسَدَ ﴾

Bismillaahir-Rahmaanir-Raheem. Qul 'a'oothu birabbil-falaq. Min sharri maa khalaq. Wa min sharri ghaasiqin 'ithaa waqab. Wa min sharrin-naffaathaati fil-'uqad. Wa min sharri haasidin 'ithaa hasad.

With the Name of Allāh, the Most Gracious, the Most Merciful. Say: I seek refuge with (Allāh) the Lord of the daybreak, from the evil of what He has created, and from the evil of the darkening (night) as it comes with its darkness, and from the evil of those who practice witchcraft when they blow in the knots, and from the evil of the envier when he envies.

بِسْمِ ٱللَّهِ ٱلرَّحْمَٰنِ ٱلرَّحِيمِ ﴿قُلْ أَعُوذُ بِرَبِّ ٱلنَّاسِ ٥مَلِكِ ٱلنَّاسِ ٥إِلَٰهِ ٱلنَّاسِ ٥ مِن شَرِّ ٱلْوَسْوَاسِ ٱلْخَنَّاسِ ٥ ٱلَّذِى يُوَسْوِسُ فِى صُدُورِ ٱلنَّاسِ ٥مِنَ ٱلْجِنَّةِ وَٱلنَّاسِ ﴾

*Bismillaahir-Rahmaanir-Raheem. Qul
'a'oothu birabbin-naas. Malikin-naas.
'Ilaahin-naas. Min sharril-waswaasil-
khannaas. Allathee yuwaswisu fee sudoorin-
naas. Minal-jinnati wannaas.*

With the Name of Allāh, the Most
Gracious, the Most Merciful. Say: I seek
refuge with (Allāh) the Lord of mankind,
the King of mankind, the God of
mankind, from the evil of the whisperer
who withdraws, who whispers in the
breasts of mankind, of jinns and men.

(Then pass your hands over as much of
your body as you can reach, beginning
with the head and the face, then the entire
front of your body. Do this three
times.)[1]

١٠٠ - ﴿اللَّهُ لَا إِلَٰهَ إِلَّا هُوَ الْحَيُّ الْقَيُّومُ لَا
تَأْخُذُهُ سِنَةٌ وَلَا نَوْمٌ لَّهُ مَا فِي السَّمَٰوَٰتِ وَمَا فِي
الْأَرْضِ مَن ذَا الَّذِي يَشْفَعُ عِندَهُ إِلَّا بِإِذْنِهِ يَعْلَمُ مَا

---

[1] Al-Bukhāri, cf. Al-Asqalāni, *Fathul-Bāri* 9/
62, and Muslim 4/1723.

بَيْنَ أَيْدِيهِمْ وَمَا خَلْفَهُمْ وَلَا يُحِيطُونَ بِشَيْءٍ مِنْ عِلْمِهِ إِلَّا بِمَا شَاءَ وَسِعَ كُرْسِيُّهُ السَّمَوَاتِ وَالْأَرْضَ وَلَا يَؤُودُهُ حِفْظُهُمَا وَهُوَ الْعَلِيُّ الْعَظِيمُ ۞

100. *Allaahu laa 'ilaaha 'illaa Huwal-Hayyul-Qayyoom, laa ta'khuthuhu sinatun wa laa nawm, lahu maa fis-samaawaati wa maa fil-'ardh, man thal-lathee yashfa'u 'indahu 'illaa bi'ithnihi, ya'lamu maa bayna 'aydeehim wa maa khalfahum, wa laa yuheetoona bishay'im-min 'ilmihi 'illaa bimaa shaa'a, wasi'a kursiyyuhus-samaawaati wal'ardha, wa laa ya'ooduhu hifdhuhumaa, wa Huwal-'Aliyyul-'Adheem.*

Allāh! There is no God but He, the Ever Living, the One Who sustains and protects all that exists. Neither slumber nor sleep overtakes Him. To Him belongs whatever is in the heavens and whatever is on the earth. Who is he that can intercede with Him except with His Permission? He knows what happens to them in this world, and what will happen to them in the Hereafter. And they will never encompass anything of His Knowledge except that which He wills. His Throne extends over the heavens and the earth, and He feels no fatigue in guarding and preserving them. And He is the Most High, the Most Great.[1]

١٠١- ﴿ءَامَنَ ٱلرَّسُولُ بِمَآ أُنزِلَ إِلَيْهِ مِن رَّبِّهِ وَٱلْمُؤْمِنُونَ كُلٌّ ءَامَنَ بِٱللَّهِ وَمَلَٰٓئِكَتِهِۦ وَكُتُبِهِۦ وَرُسُلِهِۦ لَا نُفَرِّقُ بَيْنَ أَحَدٍ مِّن رُّسُلِهِۦ وَقَالُوا سَمِعْنَا وَأَطَعْنَا غُفْرَانَكَ رَبَّنَا وَإِلَيْكَ ٱلْمَصِيرُ ○ لَا يُكَلِّفُ ٱللَّهُ نَفْسًا إِلَّا وُسْعَهَا لَهَا مَا كَسَبَتْ وَعَلَيْهَا مَا ٱكْتَسَبَتْ رَبَّنَا لَا تُؤَاخِذْنَآ إِن نَّسِينَآ أَوْ أَخْطَأْنَا رَبَّنَا وَلَا تَحْمِلْ عَلَيْنَآ إِصْرًا كَمَا حَمَلْتَهُۥ عَلَى ٱلَّذِينَ مِن قَبْلِنَا رَبَّنَا وَلَا تُحَمِّلْنَا مَا

---

[1] Al-Baqarah 2:255. Whoever reads this when he lies down to sleep will have a guardian from Allāh remain with him and Satan will not be able to come near him until he rises in the morning. See Al-Bukhārī, cf. Al-Asqalāni, Fathul-Bārī 4/487.

لَا طَاقَةَ لَنَا بِهِۦ وَاعْفُ عَنَّا وَاغْفِرْ لَنَا وَارْحَمْنَآ أَنتَ مَوْلَىٰنَا فَانصُرْنَا عَلَى ٱلْقَوْمِ ٱلْكَـٰفِرِينَ ۝

101. 'Aamanar-Rasoolu bimaa 'unzila 'ilayhi mir-Rabbihi walmu'minoon, kullun 'aamana billaahi wa malaa'ikatihi wa Kutubihi wa Rusulihi, laa nufarriqu bayna 'ahadim-mir-Rusulihi, wa qaaloo sami'naa wa 'ata'naa ghufraanaka Rabbanaa wa 'ilaykal-maseer. Laa yukallifullaahu nafsan 'illaa wus'ahaa, lahaa maa kasabat wa 'alayhaa mak-tasabat, Rabbanaa laa tu'aakhithnaa 'in naseenaa 'aw 'akhta'naa, Rabbanaa wa laa tahmil 'alaynaa 'isran kamaa hamaltahu 'alal-latheena min qablinaa, Rabbanaa wa laa tuhammilnaa maa laa taaqata lanaa bihi, wa'fu 'annaa, waghfir lanaa warhamnaa, 'Anta Mawlaanaa fansurnaa 'alal-qawmil-kaafireen.

The Messenger believes in what has been send down to him from his Lord, and so do the believers. Each one believes in Allāh, His Angels, His Books, and His Messengers. They say: "We make no distinction between any of His Messengers," and they say: "We hear, and we obey. (We seek) Your Forgiveness, our Lord, and to You is the return." Allāh burdens not a person beyond what he can bear. He gets reward for that (good) which he has earned, and he is punished for that (evil) which he has earned. Our Lord! Punish us not if we forget or fall into error. Our Lord! Lay not on us a burden like that which You did lay on those before us. Our Lord! Put not on us a burden greater than we have strength to bear. Pardon us and grant us forgiveness. Have mercy on us. You are our Protector, and help us against the disbelieving people.[1]

١٠٢-«بِاسْمِكَ رَبِّي وَضَعْتُ جَنْبِي، وَبِكَ
أَرْفَعُهُ، فَإِنْ أَمْسَكْتَ نَفْسِي فَارْحَمْهَا، وَإِنْ

---

[1] Al-Baqarah 2:285-6. These two Verses will be sufficient for anyone who recites them at night before sleeping. Al-Bukhāri, cf. Al-Asqalāni, Fathul-Bāri 9/94, Muslim 1/554.

أَرْسَلْتَهَا فَاحْفَظْهَا، بِمَا تَحْفَظُ بِهِ عِبَادَكَ الصَّالِحِينَ».

102. *Bismika Rabbee wadha'tu janbee, wa bika 'arfa'uhu, fa'in 'amsakta nafsee farhamhaa, wa 'in 'arsaltahaa fahfadhhaa, bimaa tahfadhu bihi 'ibaadakas-saaliheen.*

With Your Name[1] my Lord, I lay myself down; and with Your Name I rise. And if my soul You take, have mercy on it, and if You send it back then protect it as You protect Your righteous slaves.[2]

١٠٣-«اللَّهُمَّ إِنَّكَ خَلَقْتَ نَفْسِي وَأَنْتَ تَوَفَّاهَا، لَكَ مَمَاتُهَا وَمَحْيَاهَا، إِنْ أَحْيَيْتَهَا فَاحْفَظْهَا، وَإِنْ أَمَتَّهَا فَاغْفِرْ لَهَا. اللَّهُمَّ إِنِّي أَسْأَلُكَ الْعَافِيَةَ».

---

[1] "If any of you rises from his bed and later returns to it, let him dust off his bed with his waist garment three times and mention the Name of Allāh, for he does not know what may have entered the bed after him, and when he lies down he should say...".

[2] Al-Bukhāri 11/126 and Muslim 4/2084.

103. *Allaahumma 'innaka khalaqta nafsee wa 'Anta tawaffaahaa, laka mamaatuhaa wa mahyaahaa, 'in 'ahyaytahaa fahfadhhaa, wa 'in 'amattahaa faghfir lahaa. Allaahumma 'innee 'as'alukal-'aafiyata.*

O Allāh, You have created my soul and You take it back. Unto You is its death and its life. If You give it life then protect it, and if You cause it to die then forgive it. O Allāh, I ask You for strength.[1]

١٠٤-«اللَّهُمَّ قِنِي عَذَابَكَ يَوْمَ تَبْعَثُ عِبَادَكَ».

104. *Allaahumma qinee 'athaabaka yawma tab'athu 'ibaadaka.*

O Allāh,[2] save me from Your punishment on the Day that You resurrect Your slaves. (Recite three times in Arabic.)[3]

---

[1] Muslim 4/2083 and Ahmad 2/79.
[2] "When the Prophet ﷺ wanted to lie down to sleep, he used to place his right hand under his cheek and say..."
[3] Abu Dawud 4/311. See also Al-Albāni, *Sahih At-Tirmithi* 3/143.

١٠٥ - «بِاسْمِكِ اللَّهُمَّ أَمُوتُ وَأَحْيَا».

105. *Bismika Allaahumma 'amootu wa 'ahyaa.*

In Your Name, O Allāh, I die and I live.[1]

١٠٦ - «سُبْحَانَ اللهِ، وَالْحَمْدُ لله، وَاللهُ أَكْبَرُ».

106. *Subhaanallaahi, – Walhamdu lillaahi, – Wallaahu 'Akbar.*

Glory is to Allāh (thirty-three times in Arabic), praise is to Allāh (thirty-three times), Allāh is the Most Great (thirty-four times).[2]

١٠٧ - «اللَّهُمَّ رَبَّ السَّمْوَاتِ السَّبْعِ وَرَبَّ الْعَرْشِ

[1] Here, dying and living are metaphors for sleep and wakefulness. This explains why the normal order of these words has been reversed in this *Hadith*. In other contexts the living is mentioned before dying. See Qur'ān *Al-Baqarah* 2:258, *Aal-'Imrān* 3:156, *Al-A'raf* 7:158 among many other examples, (trans.). See also Al-Asqalāni, *Fathul-Bāri* 11/113, Muslim 4/2083.

[2] Al-Bukhāri, cf. Al-Asqalāni, *Fathul-Bāri* 7/71, Muslim 4/2091.

الْعَظِيمِ، رَبَّنَا وَرَبَّ كُلِّ شَيْءٍ، فَالِقَ الْحَبِّ
وَالنَّوَى، وَمُنْزِلَ التَّوْرَاةِ وَالْإِنْجِيلِ، وَالْفُرْقَانِ،
أَعُوذُ بِكَ مِنْ شَرِّ كُلِّ شَيْءٍ أَنْتَ آخِذٌ بِنَاصِيَتِهِ.
اللَّهُمَّ أَنْتَ الْأَوَّلُ فَلَيْسَ قَبْلَكَ شَيْءٌ، وَأَنْتَ
الْآخِرُ فَلَيْسَ بَعْدَكَ شَيْءٌ، وَأَنْتَ الظَّاهِرُ فَلَيْسَ
فَوْقَكَ شَيْءٌ، وَأَنْتَ الْبَاطِنُ فَلَيْسَ دُونَكَ شَيْءٌ،
اقْضِ عَنَّا الدَّيْنَ وَأَغْنِنَا مِنَ الْفَقْرِ».

107. *Allaahumma Rabbas-samaawaatis-sab'i
wa Rabbal-'Arshil-'Adheem, Rabbanaa wa
Rabba kulli shay'in, faaliqal-habbi wannawaa,
wa munzilat-Tawraati wal-'Injeeli, wal-
Furqaani, 'a'oothu bika min sharri kulli
shay'in 'Anta 'aakhithun binaasiyatihi.
Allaahumma 'Antal-'Awwalu falaysa qablaka
shay'un, wa 'Antal-'Aakhiru falaysa ba'daka
shay'un, wa 'Antadh-Dhaahiru falaysa
fawqaka shay'un, wa 'Antal-Baatinu falaysa
doonaka shay'un, iqdhi 'annad-dayna wa
'aghninaa minal-faqri.*

O Allāh! Lord of the seven heavens and Lord of the Magnificent Throne. Our Lord and the Lord of everything. Splitter of the grain and the date-stone, Revealer of the Torah and the Injeel[1] and the *Furqān* (the Qur'ān), I seek refuge in You from the evil of everything that You shall seize by the forelock.[2] O Allāh You are the First and nothing has come before you, and You are the Last, and nothing may come after You. You are the Most High, nothing is above You and You are the Most Near and nothing is nearer than You. Remove our debts from us and enrich us against poverty.[3]

١٠٨ -«الْحَمْدُ للهِ الَّذِي أَطْعَمَنَا وَسَقَانَا، وَكَفَانَا، وَآوَانَا، فَكُمْ مِمَّنْ لَا كَافِيَ لَهُ وَلَا مُؤْوِيَ».

---

[1] The Scripture that was revealed to 'Īsa (Jesus).

[2] See Qur'ān Al-'Alaq 96:15, where seizure by the forelock preceeds being cast into Hell. (Translator)

[3] Muslim 4/2084.

108. *Alhamdu lillaahil-lathee 'at'amanaa wa saqaanaa, wa kafaanaa, wa 'aawaanaa, fakam mimman laa kaafiya lahu wa laa mu'wiya.*

Praise is to Allāh Who has provided us with food and with drink, sufficed us and gave us an abode, for how many are there with no provision and with no home.[1]

١٠٩-«اللَّهُمَّ عَالِمَ الْغَيْبِ وَالشَّهَادَةِ فَاطِرَ السَّمَوَاتِ وَالْأَرْضِ، رَبَّ كُلِّ شَيْءٍ وَمَلِيكَهُ، أَشْهَدُ أَنْ لَا إِلَهَ إِلَّا أَنْتَ، أَعُوذُ بِكَ مِنْ شَرِّ نَفْسِي، وَمِنْ شَرِّ الشَّيْطَانِ وَشِرْكِهِ، وَأَنْ أَقْتَرِفَ عَلَى نَفْسِي سُوءًا، أَوْ أَجُرَّهُ إِلَى مُسْلِمٍ».

109. *Allaahumma 'Aalimal-ghaybi wash-shahaadati faatiras-samaawaati wal'ardhi, Rabba kulli shay'in wa maleekahu, 'ash-hadu 'an laa 'ilaaha 'illaa 'Anta, 'a'oothu bika min sharri nafsee, wa min sharrish- shaytaani wa shirkihi, wa 'an 'aqtarifa 'alaa nafsee soo'an, 'aw 'ajurrahu 'ilaa Muslimin.*

---

[1] Muslim 4/2085.

O Allāh, Knower of the unseen and the evident, Maker of the heavens and the earth, Lord of everything and its Master, I bear witness that there is none worthy of worship but You. I seek refuge in You from the evil of my soul and from the evil of Satan and his helpers. (I seek refuge in You) from bringing evil upon my soul and from harming any Muslim.[1]

١١٠-﴿الٓمّٓ ○ تَنزِيلُ ٱلْكِتَٰبِ﴾ وَ ﴿تَبَٰرَكَ ٱلَّذِى بِيَدِهِ ٱلْمُلْكُ﴾ .

110. Recite *Surah* 32 (*As-Sajdah*) and *Surah* 67 (*Al-Mulk*) in Arabic.[2]

١١١-«اللَّهُمَّ أَسْلَمْتُ نَفْسِي إِلَيْكَ، وَفَوَّضْتُ أَمْرِي إِلَيْكَ، وَوَجَّهْتُ وَجْهِي إِلَيْكَ، وَأَلْجَأْتُ ظَهْرِي إِلَيْكَ، رَغْبَةً وَرَهْبَةً إِلَيْكَ، لَا مَلْجَأَ وَلَا

[1] Abu Dawud 4/317. See also Al-Albāni, *Sahih At-Tirmithi* 3/142.
[2] At-Tirmithi, An-Nasā'i. See also Al-Albāni, *Sahihul-Jāmi' As-Saghir* 4/255.

مَنْجَا مِنْكَ إِلَّا إِلَيْكَ، آمَنْتُ بِكِتَابِكَ الَّذِي
أَنْزَلْتَ وَبِنَبِيِّكَ الَّذِي أَرْسَلْتَ».

111. *Allaahumma 'aslamtu nafsee 'ilayka, wa
fawwadhtu 'amree 'ilayka, wa wajjahtu
wajhee 'ilayka, wa 'alja'tu dhahree 'ilayka,
raghbatan wa rahbatan 'ilayka, laa malja' wa
laa manja minka 'illaa 'ilayka, 'aamantu
bikitaabikal-lathee 'anzalta wa bi-nabiyyikal-
lathee 'arsalta.*

O Allāh,[1] I submit myself to You,
entrust my affairs to You, turn my face to
You, and lay myself down depending
upon You, hoping in You and fearing
You. There is no refuge, and no escape,
except to You. I believe in Your Book (the
Qur'ān) that You revealed, and the
Prophet whom You sent.[2]

---

[1] "Before you go to bed perform ablutions as
you would for prayer, then lie down on your
right side and say..."
[2] The Prophet ﷺ said: "Whoever says this
and dies in his sleep, has died in a state of the

29. Invocation to say if you stir in the night

١١٢-«لَا إِلَهَ إِلَّا اللهُ الْوَاحِدُ الْقَهَّارُ، رَبُّ
السَّمَوَاتِ وَالْأَرْضِ وَمَا بَيْنَهُمَا الْعَزِيزُ
الْغَفَّارُ».

112. *Laa 'ilaaha 'illallaahul-Waahidul-Qahhaaru, Rabbus-samaawaati wal'ardhi wa maa baynahumal-'Azeezul-Ghaffaaru.*

There is none worthy of worship but Allāh, the One, the Victorious, Lord of the heavens and the earth and all that is between them, the All-Mighty, the All-Forgiving.[1]

---

natural monotheism (*Fitrah*)." Al-Bukhāri, cf. Al-Asqalāni, *Fathul-Bāri* 11/113, Muslim 4/2081.

[1] This is to be said if you turn over in bed during the night. Al-Hākim graded it authentic and Ath-Thahabi agreed 1/540. Also see An-Nasā'i, *'Amalul-Yawm wal-Laylah,* and Ibn As-Sunni. See also Al-Albāni, *Sahihul-Jāmi' As-Saghīr* 4/213.

30. What to say if you are afraid to go to sleep or feel lonely and depressed

١١٣ -«أَعُوذُ بِكَلِمَاتِ اللهِ التَّامَّاتِ مِنْ غَضَبِهِ
وَعِقَابِهِ، وَشَرِّ عِبَادِهِ، وَمِنْ هَمَزَاتِ الشَّيَاطِينِ
وَأَنْ يَحْضُرُونِ».

113. 'A'oothu bikalimaatil-laahit-taammaati min ghadhabihi wa 'iqaabihi, wa sharri 'ibaadihi, wa min hamazaatish-shayaateeni wa 'an yahdhuroon.

I seek refuge in the Perfect Words of Allāh from His anger and His punishment, from the evil of His slaves and from the taunts of devils and from their presence.[1]

31. What to do if you have a bad dream or nightmare

114. Spit to your left (three times).[2]

---

[1] Abu Dawud 4/12. See also Al-Albāni, *Sahih At-Tirmithi* 3/171.
[2] Muslim 4/1772.

Seek refuge in Allāh from the Devil and from the evil of what you have seen (three times).[1]

Do not speak about it to anyone.[2]

Turn over on your other side.[3]

115. Get up and pray if you desire to do so.[4]

32. Invocations for *Qunut* in the *Witr* prayer

١١٦-«اللَّهُمَّ اهْدِنِي فِيمَنْ هَدَيْتَ، وَعَافِنِي فِيمَنْ عَافَيْتَ، وَتَوَلَّنِي فِيمَنْ تَوَلَّيْتَ، وَبَارِكْ لِي فِيمَا أَعْطَيْتَ، وَقِنِي شَرَّ مَا قَضَيْتَ، فَإِنَّكَ تَقْضِي وَلَا يُقْضَى عَلَيْكَ، إِنَّهُ لَا يَذِلُّ مَنْ وَالَيْتَ، [وَلَا يَعِزُّ مَنْ عَادَيْتَ]، تَبَارَكْتَ رَبَّنَا وَتَعَالَيْتَ».

---

[1] Muslim 4/1772,3.
[2] Muslim 4/1772.
[3] Muslim 4/1773.
[4] Muslim 4/1773.

116. *Allaahum-mahdinee feeman hadayta, wa 'aafinee feeman 'aafayta, wa tawallanee feeman tawallayta, wa baarik lee feemaa 'a'atayta, wa qinee sharra maa qadhayta, fa'innaka taqdhee wa laa yuqdhaa 'alayka, 'innahu laa yathillu man waalayta, [wa laa ya 'izzu man 'aadayta], tabaarakta Rabbanaa wa ta'aalayta.*

O Allāh, guide me with those whom You have guided, and strengthen me with those whom You have given strength. Take me to Your care with those whom You have taken to Your care. Bless me in what You have given me. Protect me from the evil You have ordained. Surely, You command and are not commanded, and none whom You have committed to Your care shall be humiliated [and none whom You have taken as an enemy shall taste glory]. You are Blessed, Our Lord, and Exalted.[1]

---

[1] Abu Dawud, Ibn Mājah, An-Nasā'i, At-Tirmithi, Ahmad, Ad-Dārimi, Al-Hākim, and Al-Bayhaqi. See also Al-Albāni, *Sahih At-Tirmithi* 1/144, *Sahih Ibn Mājah* 1/194, and *'Irwā'ul-Ghalīl* 2/172.

١١٧-«اللَّهُمَّ إِنِّي أَعُوذُ بِرِضَاكَ مِنْ سَخَطِكَ، وَبِمُعَافَاتِكَ مِنْ عُقُوبَتِكَ، وَأَعُوذُ بِكَ مِنْكَ، لَا أُحْصِي ثَنَاءً عَلَيْكَ، أَنْتَ كَمَا أَثْنَيْتَ عَلَى نَفْسِكَ».

117. *Allaahumma 'innee 'a'oothu biridhaaka min sakhatika, wa bimu'aafaatika min 'uqoobatika, wa 'a'oothu bika minka, laa 'uhsee thanaa'an 'alayka, 'Anta kamaa 'athnayta 'alaa nafsika.*

O Allāh, I seek refuge with Your Pleasure from Your anger. I seek refuge in Your forgiveness from Your punishment. I seek refuge in You from You. I cannot count Your praises, You are as You have praised Yourself.[1]

١١٨-«اللَّهُمَّ إِيَّاكَ نَعْبُدُ، وَلَكَ نُصَلِّي وَنَسْجُدُ،

---

[1] Abu Dawud, Ibn Mājah, An-Nasā'i, At-Tirmithi, Ahmad. See Al-Albāni, *Sahih At-Tirmithi* 3/180, *Sahih Ibn Mājah* 1/194, and *'Irwā'ul-Ghalīl* 2/175.

وَإِلَيْكَ نَسْعَى وَنَحْفِدُ، نَرْجُو رَحْمَتَكَ،
وَنَخْشَى عَذَابَكَ، إِنَّ عَذَابَكَ بِالْكَافِرِينَ
مُلْحَقٌ. اللَّهُمَّ إِنَّا نَسْتَعِينُكَ، وَنَسْتَغْفِرُكَ،
وَنُثْنِي عَلَيْكَ الْخَيْرَ، وَلَا نَكْفُرُكَ، وَنُؤْمِنُ
بِكَ، وَنَخْضَعُ لَكَ، وَنَخْلَعُ مَنْ يَكْفُرُكَ».

118. *Allaahumma 'iyyaaka na'budu, wa laka
nusallee wa nasjudu, wa 'ilayka nas'aa wa
nahfidu, narjoo rahmataka, wa nakhshaa
'athaabaka, 'inna 'athaabaka bilkaafireena
mulhaq. Allaahumma 'innaa nasta'eenuka,
wa nastaghfiruka, wa nuthnee 'alaykal-khayr,
wa laa nakfuruka, wa nu'minu bika, wa
nakhdha'u laka, wa nakhla'u man yakfuruka.*

O Allāh, You alone do we worship and to
You we pray and bow down prostrate. To
You we hasten to worship and to serve.
Our hope is for Your mercy and we fear
Your punishment. Surely, Your
punishment of the disbelievers is at hand.
O Allāh, we seek Your help and Your

forgiveness, and we praise You beneficently. We do not deny You and we believe in You. We surrender to You and renounce whoever disbelieves in You.[1]

33. What to say immediately following the *Witr* prayer

١١٩-«سُبْحَانَ الْمَلِكِ الْقُدُّوسِ» .

119. *Subhaanal-Malikil-Quddoosi.*

Glory is to the King, the Holy. [Recite three times in Arabic, and raise and extend the voice on the third time and say...]

«رَبِّ الْمَلَائِكَةِ وَالرُّوحِ» .

Rabbil-malaa'ikati warroohi.

Lord of the angels and the Spirit.[2]

---

[1] Al-Bayhaqi graded its chain authentic in *As-Sunan Al-Kubrā*. Al-Albāni said in *'Irwā'ul-Ghalīl* 2/170 that its chain is authentic as a statement of 'Umar.
[2] An-Nasā'i 3/244, Ad-Dāraqutni and others. The final addition is from Ad-Dāraqutni's

34. Invocations in times of worry and grief

١٢٠-«اللَّهُمَّ إِنِّي عَبْدُكَ، ابْنُ عَبْدِكَ، ابْنُ
أَمَتِكَ، نَاصِيَتِي بِيَدِكَ، مَاضٍ فِيَّ حُكْمُكَ،
عَدْلٌ فِيَّ قَضَاؤُكَ، أَسْأَلُكَ بِكُلِّ اسْمٍ هُوَ لَكَ،
سَمَّيْتَ بِهِ نَفْسَكَ، أَوْ أَنْزَلْتَهُ فِي كِتَابِكَ، أَوْ
عَلَّمْتَهُ أَحَدًا مِنْ خَلْقِكَ، أَوِ اسْتَأْثَرْتَ بِهِ فِي
عِلْمِ الْغَيْبِ عِنْدَكَ، أَنْ تَجْعَلَ الْقُرْآنَ رَبِيعَ
قَلْبِي، وَنُورَ صَدْرِي، وَجَلَاءَ حُزْنِي، وَذَهَابَ
هَمِّي».

120. *Allaahumma 'innee 'abduka, ibnu
'abdika, ibnu 'amatika, naasiyatee biyadika,
maadhin fiyya hukmuka, 'adlun fiyya
qadhaa'uka, 'as'aluka bikulli ismin huwa laka,
sammayta bihi nafsaka, 'aw 'anzaltahu fee*

version 2/31 and its chain of narration is
authentic. See the checking of *Zādul-Ma'ād* by
Shu'aib Al-Arna'ut and 'Abdul-Qādir Al-
Arna'ut 1/337.

kitaabika, 'aw 'allamtahu 'ahadan min khalqika, 'awista'tharta bihi fee 'ilmil-ghaybi 'indaka, 'an taj'alal-Qur'aana rabee'a qalbee, wa noora sadree, wa jalaa'a huznee, wa thahaaba hammee.

O Allāh, I am Your slave and the son of Your male slave and the son of your female slave. My forehead is in Your Hand (i.e. you have control over me). Your Judgment upon me is assured and Your Decree concerning me is just. I ask You by every Name that You have named Yourself with, revealed in Your Book, taught any one of Your creation or kept unto Yourself in the knowledge of the unseen that is with You, to make the Qur'ān the spring of my heart, and the light of my chest, the banisher of my sadness and the reliever of my distress.[1]

١٢١ –«اللَّهُمَّ إِنِّي أَعُوذُ بِكَ مِنَ الْهَمِّ وَالْحَزَنِ،

---

[1] Ahmad 1/391, and Al-Albāni graded it authentic.

141

وَالْعَجْزِ وَالْكَسَلِ، وَالْبُخْلِ وَالْجُبْنِ، وَضَلَعِ الدَّيْنِ وَغَلَبَةِ الرِّجَالِ».

121. *Allaahumma 'innee 'a'oothu bika minal-hammi walhazani, wal'ajzi walkasali, walbukhli waljubni, wa dhala'id-dayni wa ghalabatir-rijaal.*

O Allāh, I seek refuge in you from grief and sadness, from weakness and from laziness, from miserliness and from cowardice, from being overcome by debt and overpowered by men (i.e. others).[1]

35. Invocations for anguish

١٢٢-«لَا إِلَهَ إِلَّا اللهُ الْعَظِيمُ الْحَلِيمُ، لَا إِلَهَ إِلَّا اللهُ رَبُّ الْعَرْشِ الْعَظِيمِ، لَا إِلَهَ إِلَّا اللهُ رَبُّ السَّمْوَاتِ وَرَبُّ الأَرْضِ وَرَبُّ الْعَرْشِ الْكَرِيمِ»

122. *Laa 'ilaaha 'illallaahul-'Adheemul-*

---

[1] Al-Bukhāri 7/158. See also Al-Asqalāni, *Fathul-Bāri* 11/173.

Haleem, laa 'ilaaha 'illallaahu Rabbul-'Arshil-'Adheem, laa 'ilaaha 'illallaahu Rabbus-samaawaati wa Rabbul-'ardhi wa Rabbul-'Arshil-Kareem.

There is none worthy of worship but Allāh the Mighty, the Forbearing. There is none worthy of worship but Allāh, Lord of the Magnificent Throne. There is none worthy of worship but Allāh, Lord of the heavens and Lord of the earth, and Lord of the Noble Throne.[1]

١٢٣-«اللَّهُمَّ رَحْمَتَكَ أَرْجُو فَلَا تَكِلْنِي إِلَى نَفْسِي طَرْفَةَ عَيْنٍ، وَأَصْلِحْ لِي شَأْنِي كُلَّهُ، لَا إِلَهَ إِلَّا أَنْتَ».

123. *Allaahumma rahmataka 'arjoo falaa takilnee 'ilaa nafsee tarfata 'aynin, wa 'aslih lee sha'nee kullahu, laa'ilaaha 'illaa 'Anta.*

O Allāh, I hope for Your mercy. Do not leave me to myself even for the blinking of an eye (i.e. a moment). Correct all of

---

[1] Al-Bukhāri 8/154, Muslim 4/2092.

my affairs for me. There is none worthy of worship but You.[1]

١٢٤-«لَا إِلَهَ إِلَّا أَنْتَ سُبْحَانَكَ إِنِّي كُنْتُ مِنَ الظَّالِمِينَ» .

124. Laa 'ilaaha 'illaa 'Anta subhaanaka 'innee kuntu minadh-dhaalimeen.

There is none worthy of worship but You, glory is to You. Surely, I was among the wrongdoers.[2]

١٢٥-«اللهُ اللهُ رَبِّي لَا أُشْرِكُ بِهِ شَيْئًا» .

125. Allaahu Allaahu Rabbee laa 'ushriku bihi shay'an.

Allāh, Allāh is my Lord. I do not associate anything with Him.[3]

---

[1] Abu Dawud 4/324, Ahmad 5/42. Al-Albāni graded it as good in Sahih Abu Dawud 3/959.
[2] At-Tirmithi 5/529. Al-Hākim declared it authentic and Ath-Thahabi agreed with him 1/505. See also Al-Albāni, Sahih At-Tirmithi 3/168.
[3] Abu Dawud 2/87. See also Al-Albāni, Sahih Ibn Mājah 2/335.

36. Invocations for when you meet an adversary or a powerful ruler

١٢٦-«اللَّهُمَّ إِنَّا نَجْعَلُكَ فِي نُحُورِهِمْ وَنَعُوذُ بِكَ مِنْ شُرُورِهِمْ».

126. *Allaahumma 'innaa naj'aluka fee nuhoorihim wa na'oothu bika min shuroorihim.*

O Allāh, we ask You to restrain them by their necks and we seek refuge in You from their evil.[1]

١٢٧-«اللَّهُمَّ أَنْتَ عَضُدِي، وَأَنْتَ نَصِيرِي، بِكَ أَجُولُ، وَبِكَ أَصُولُ، وَبِكَ أُقَاتِلُ».

127. *Allaahumma 'Anta 'adhudee, wa 'Anta naseeree, bika 'ajoolu, wa bika 'asoolu, wa bika 'uqaatilu.*

O Allāh, You are my strength and You are my support. For Your sake I go forth and for Your sake I advance and for Your

---

[1] Abu Dawud 2/89, and Al-Hākim graded it authentic and Ath-Thahabi agreed 2/142.

sake I fight.[1]

١٢٨-«حَسْبُنَا اللهُ وَنِعْمَ الْوَكِيلُ».

128. *Hasbunallaahu wa ni'amal-wakeel.*

Allāh is sufficient for us and the best of those on whom to depend.[2]

37. Invocations against the oppression of rulers

١٢٩-«اللَّهُمَّ رَبَّ السَّمْوَاتِ السَّبْعِ، وَرَبَّ الْعَرْشِ الْعَظِيمِ، كُنْ لِي جَارًا مِنْ فُلَانِ بْنِ فُلَانٍ، وَأَحْزَابِهِ مِنْ خَلَائِقِكَ؛ أَنْ يَفْرُطَ عَلَيَّ أَحَدٌ مِنْهُمْ أَوْ يَطْغَى، عَزَّ جَارُكَ، وَجَلَّ ثَنَاؤُكَ، وَلَا إِلَهَ إِلَّا أَنْتَ».

129. *Allaahumma Rabbas-samaawaatis-sab'i, wa Rabbal-'Arshil-'Adheem, kun lee jaaran min [here you mention the person's name], wa 'ahzaabihi min khalaa'iqika, 'an*

---

[1] Abu Dawud 3/42, At-Tirmithi 5/572. See also Al-Albāni, *Sahih At-Tirmithi* 3/183.

[2] Al-Bukhāri, 5/172.

*yafruta 'alayya 'ahadun minhum 'aw
yatghaa, 'azza jaaruka, wa jalla thanaa'uka,
wa laa 'ilaaha 'illaa 'Anta.*

O Allāh, Lord of the seven heavens, Lord
of the Magnificent Throne, be for me a
support against [*such and such a person*]
and his helpers from among your
creatures, lest any of them abuse me or do
me wrong. Mighty is Your patronage and
glorious are Your praises. There is none
worthy of worship but You.[1]

١٣٠- «اللهُ أَكْبَرُ، اللهُ أَعَزُّ مِنْ خَلْقِهِ جَمِيعًا،
اللهُ أَعَزُّ مِمَّا أَخَافُ وَأَحْذَرُ، أَعُوذُ بِاللهِ الَّذِي
لَا إِلَهَ إِلَّا هُوَ، الْمُمْسِكِ السَّمَوَاتِ السَّبْعِ أَنْ
يَقَعْنَ عَلَى الْأَرْضِ إِلَّا بِإِذْنِهِ، مِنْ شَرِّ عَبْدِكَ
فُلَانٍ، وَجُنُودِهِ وَأَتْبَاعِهِ وَأَشْيَاعِهِ، مِنَ الْجِنِّ
وَالْإِنْسِ، اللَّهُمَّ كُنْ لِي جَارًا مِنْ شَرِّهِمْ، جَلَّ

[1] Al-Bukhāri, *Al-'Adab Al-Mufrad* (no. 707).
Al-Albāni graded it authentic in *Sahih Al-'Adab
Al-Mufrad* (no. 545).

ثَنَاؤُكَ وَعَزَّ جَارُكَ، وَتَبَارَكَ اسْمُكَ، وَلَا إِلَهَ
غَيْرُكَ» .

130. *Allaahu 'Akbar, Allahu 'a'azzu min khalqihi jamee'an, Allaahu 'a'azzu mimmaa 'akhaafu wa 'ahtharu, 'a'oothu billaahil-lathee laa 'ilaaha 'illaa Huwa, almumsikis-samaawaatis-sab'i 'an yaqa'na 'alal-'ardhi 'illaa bi'ithnihi, min sharri 'abdika [name of the person], wa junoodihi wa 'atbaa'ihi wa 'ashyaa'ihi, minal-jinni wal'insi, Allaahumma kun lee jaaran min sharrihim, jalla thanaa'uka wa 'azza jaaruka, wa tabaarakasmuka, wa laa 'ilaaha ghayruka.*

Allāh is the Most Great, Mightier than all His creation. He is Mightier than what I fear and dread. I seek refuge in Allāh, Who there is none worthy of worship but Him. He is the One Who holds the seven heavens from falling upon the earth except by His command. [I seek refuge in You Allāh] from the evil of Your slave [*name of the person*], and his helpers, his followers and his supporters from among the jinn and mankind. O Allāh, be my support against their evil. Glorious are Your praises and mighty is Your patronage. Blessed is Your Name, there is no true God but You. (Recite three times in Arabic.)[1]

38. Invocation against an enemy

١٣١ –«اللَّهُمَّ مُنْزِلَ الْكِتَابِ، سَرِيعَ الْحِسَابِ، اهْزِمِ الْأَحْزَابَ، اللَّهُمَّ اهْزِمْهُمْ وَزَلْزِلْهُمْ» .

131. Allaahumma munzilal-kitaabi, saree'al-hisaabi, ihzimil-'ahzaaba, Allaahumma ihzimhum wa zalzilhum.

O Allāh, Revealer of the Book, Swift to account, defeat the groups (of disbelievers). O Allāh, defeat them and shake them.[2]

---

[1] Al-Bukhāri, Al-'Adab Al-Mufrad (no. 708). Al-Albāni graded it authentic in Sahih Al-'Adab Al-Mufrad (no. 546).
[2] Muslim 3/1362.

39. What to say if you fear people may harm you

١٣٢ –«اللَّهُمَّ اكْفِنِهِمْ بِمَا شِئْتَ» .

132. Allaahummak-fineehim bimaa shi'ta.

O Allāh, suffice (i.e. protect) me against them however You wish.[1]

40. Invocations for if you are stricken by in your faith

133. (Say:) I seek refuge in Allāh. (Then you should desist from doing what you are in doubt about.)[2]

١٣٤ –«آمَنْتُ بِاللهِ وَرُسُلِهِ» .

134. 'Aamantu billaahi wa Rusulihi.

(Say:) I believe in Allāh and His Messenger.[3]

١٣٥ –﴿هُوَ الْأَوَّلُ وَالْآخِرُ وَالظَّاهِرُ وَالْبَاطِنُ وَهُوَ بِكُلِّ شَيْءٍ عَلِيمٌ﴾

---

[1] Muslim 4/2300.
[2] Al-Bukhāri, cf. Al-Asqalāni, Fathul-Bāri 6/336, Muslim 1/120.
[3] Muslim, 1/119-20.

135. *Huwal-'Awwalu wal-'Aakhiru wadh-Dhaahiru wal-Baatinu, wa Huwa bikulli shay'in 'Aleem.*

(Recite the *Ayat*:) He is the First and the Last, the Most High and the Most Near. And He is the Knower of all things (in Arabic).[1]

41. Invocations for the setting of a debt

١٣٦ - «اللَّهُمَّ اكْفِنِي بِحَلَالِكَ عَنْ حَرَامِكَ وَأَغْنِنِي بِفَضْلِكَ عَمَّنْ سِوَاكَ».

136. *Allaahummak-finee bihalaalika 'an haraamika wa 'aghninee bifadhlika 'amman siwaaka.*

O Allāh, suffice me with what You have allowed instead of what You have forbidden, and make me independent of all others besides You.[2]

---

[1] *Al-Hadid* 57:3, Abu Dawud 4/329. Al-Albāni graded it good in *Sahih Abu Dawud,* 3/962.

[2] At-Tirmithi 5/560. See also Al-Albāni, *Sahih At-Tirmithi* 3/180.

١٣٧-«اللّهُمَّ إِنِّي أَعُوذُ بِكَ مِنَ الْهَمِّ وَالْحَزَنِ، وَالْعَجْزِ وَالْكَسَلِ، وَالْبُخْلِ وَالْجُبْنِ، وَضَلَعِ الدَّيْنِ وَغَلَبَةِ الرِّجَالِ».

137. Allaahumma 'innee 'a'oothu bika minal-hammi walhazani, wal'ajzi walkasali, walbukhli waljubni, wa dhala'id-dayni wa ghalabatir-rijaali.

O Allāh, I seek refuge in You from grief and sadness, from weakness and from laziness, from miserliness and from cowardice, from being overcome by debt and from being overpowered by men (i.e. other people).[1]

42. Invocation against the distractions of Satan during the prayer and recitation of the Qur'ān

١٣٨-«أَعُوذُ بِاللهِ مِنَ الشَّيْطَانِ الرَّجِيمِ».

138. 'A'oothu billaahi minash-Shaytaanir-rajeem.

---

[1] Al-Bukhāri 7/158.

(Say:) I seek refuge in Allāh from Satan the outcast (then spit to your left). (Do this three times reciting in Arabic.)[1]

43. Invocation for when you find something becoming difficult for you

١٣٩-«اللَّهُمَّ لَا سَهْلَ إِلَّا مَا جَعَلْتَهُ سَهْلًا وَأَنْتَ تَجْعَلُ الْحَزْنَ إِذَا شِئْتَ سَهْلًا».

139. *Allaahumma laa sahla 'illaa maa ja'altahu sahlan wa 'Anta taj'alul-hazna 'ithaa shi'ta sahlan.*

O Allāh, there is no ease other than what You make easy. If You please You ease sorrow.[2]

---

[1] Muslim 4/1729.
[2] Ibn Hibban in his *Sahih* (no. 2427), and Ibn As-Sunni (no. 351). Al-Hāfidh (Ibn Hajar) said that this *Hadith* is authentic. It was also declared authentic by 'Abdul-Qādir Al-Arna'ut in his checking of An-Nawawi's *Kitābul-Athkār* p. 106.

44. What to say and do if you commit a sin

140. There is not any slave of Allāh who commits a sin, then he perfects his ablution and stands to pray two *Rak'ahs* of prayer, then seeks Allāh's forgiveness, except that Allāh will forgive him.[1]

45. Invocations against the Devil and his promptings

141. Seeking refuge with Allāh against him (i.e. by saying I seek refuge in Allāh from Satan the outcast).[2]

142. The call to prayer – 'Athān.[3]

143. Saying words of Allāh's remembrance (*Thikr*) and recitation of the Qur'ān.[4]

---

[1] Abu Dawud 2/86, At-Tirmithi 2/257. Al-Albāni graded it authentic in *Sahih Abu Dawud* 1/283.

[2] Abu Dawud 1/206, At-Tirmithi. See also Al-Albāni, *Sahih At-Tirmithi* 1/77, and *Surat Al-Mu'minûn*, 23:98-9.

[3] Muslim 1/291, Al-Bukhāri 1/151.

[4] "Do not turn your homes into graveyards,

46. Invocation for when something you dislike happens, or for when you fail to achieve what you attempt to do

١٤٤ - «قَدَرُ اللهِ وَمَا شَاءَ فَعَلَ».

144. *Qadarullaahi wa maa shaa'a fa'ala.*

It is the Decree of Allāh and He does whatever He Wills.[1]

---

surely the Devil flees from the house in which *Surat Al-Baqarah* is read," Muslim 1/539. The Devil is also driven out by the invocations for morning and evening, those that are said before sleeping and upon waking up, those for entering and leaving the house, including those for entering and leaving the mosque, and by many other authentic invocations taught to us by the Prophet ﷺsuch as the reading of *'Āyatul-Kursi*, (*Al-Baqarah* 2:255), and the last two *'Āyat* of *Surat Al-Baqarah* before going to sleep. Whoever says: "There is none worthy of worship but Allāh alone, Who has no partner, His is the dominion and His is the praise, and he is Able to do all things," one hundred times, it will be a protection for him from the Devil throughout the day.

[1] "The strong believer is better and more dear

47. Congratulations for new parents and how they should respond

١٤٥-«بَارَكَ اللهُ لَكَ فِي الْمَوْهُوبِ لَكَ، وَشَكَرْتَ الْوَاهِبَ، وَبَلَغَ أَشُدَّهُ، وَرُزِقْتَ بِرَّهُ».

145. *Baarakallaahu laka fil-mawhoobi laka, wa shakartal-waahiba, wa balagha 'ashuddahu, wa ruziqta birrahu.*

May Allāh bless you with His gift to you, and may you (the new parent) give thanks, may the child reach the maturity of years, and may you be granted its righteousness.

The reply of the person being congratulated is to say:

«بَارَكَ اللهُ لَكَ وَبَارَكَ عَلَيْكَ، وَجَزَاكَ اللهُ خَيْرًا، وَرَزَقَكَ اللهُ مِثْلَهُ، وَأَجْزَلَ ثَوَابَكَ»

Baarakallahu laka wa baaraka 'alayka, wa jazaakallaahu khayran, wa razaqakallaahu mithlahu, wa 'ajzala thawaabaka.

May Allāh bless you, and shower His

blessings upon you, and may Allāh reward you well and bestow upon you its like and reward you abundantly.[1]

48. How to seek Allāh's protection for children

The Prophet ﷺ used to seek Allāh's protection for Al-Hasan and Al-Husain by saying:

١٤٦-«أُعِيذُكُمَا بِكَلِمَاتِ اللهِ التَّامَّةِ مِنْ كُلِّ شَيْطَانٍ وَهَامَّةٍ، وَمِنْ كُلِّ عَيْنٍ لَامَّةٍ».

146. *'U'eethukumaa bikalimaatil-laahit-*

---

to Allāh than the weak believer, and in each of them there is good. Be vigilant for what is to your benefit and seek the help of Allāh and do not falter. But when you are striken by some setback, do not say: 'If only I had done such and such,' rather say: 'It is the Decree of Allāh and He does whatever He wills.' For verily the saying 'if' (i.e. if only I had) begins the work of the Devil." Muslim 4/2052.

[1] An-Nawawi, *Kitābul-'Athkār* p. 349, and *Sahihul-'Athkār* 2/713 by Saleem Al-Hilāli.

taammati min kulli shaytaanin wa haammatin, wa min kulli 'aynin laammatin.

I seek protection for you in the Perfect Words of Allāh from every devil and every beast, and from every envious blameworthy eye.[1]

49. Invocations for visiting the sick

١٤٧–«لَا بَأْسَ طَهُورٌ إِنْ شَاءَ اللهُ»

147. *Laa ba'sa tahoorun 'in shaa' Allaah.*

Do not worry, it will be a purification (for you), Allāh willing.[2]

١٤٨–«أَسْأَلُ اللهَ الْعَظِيمَ رَبَّ الْعَرْشِ الْعَظِيمِ أَنْ يَشْفِيَكَ».

148. *'As'alullaahal-'Adheema Rabbal-'Arshil-'Adheemi 'an yashfiyaka.*

I ask Almighty Allāh, Lord of the Magnificent Throne, to make you well.

---

[1] Al-Bukhāri 4/119.

[2] Al-Bukhāri, cf. Al-Asqalāni *Fathul-Bāri* 10/118.

158

(Recite seven times in Arabic.)[1]

50. The reward for visiting the sick

149. When a man goes to visit his sick Muslim brother, he walks along a path of Paradise until he sits, and when he sits he is cloaked in mercy. If he comes in the morning, seventy thousand angels pray for him until evening, and if he comes in the evening, seventy thousand angels pray for him until morning.[2]

51. Invocations of the terminally ill

١٥٠-«اللَّهُمَّ اغْفِرْ لِي وَارْحَمْنِي وَأَلْحِقْنِي بِالرَّفِيقِ الأَعْلَى».

150. *Allaahum-maghfir lee warhamnee wa*

---

[1] At-Tirmithi, Abu Dawud. See also Al-Albāni, *Sahih At-Tirmithi* 2/210 and *Sahihul-Jāmi' As-Saghir* 5/180.

[2] At-Tirmithi, Ibn Mājah, Ahmad. See Al-Albāni, *Sahih Ibn Mājah* 1/244, and *Sahih At-Tirmithi* 1/286. It was also graded authentic by Ahmad Shākir.

'alhiqnee bir-rafeeqil-'a'laa.

O Allāh, forgive me and have mercy upon me and join me with the highest companions (in Paradise).[1]

As he was dying, the Prophet ﷺ dipped his hands in water and wiped his face saying:

١٥١-«لَا إِلَهَ إِلَّا اللهُ إِنَّ لِلْمَوْتِ لَسَكَرَاتٍ».

151. *Laa 'ilaaha 'illallaahu 'inna lilmawti lasakaraatin.*

There is none worthy of worship but Allāh, surely death has agonies.[2]

١٥٢-لَا إِلَهَ إِلَّا اللهُ وَاللهُ أَكْبَرُ، لَا إِلَهَ إِلَّا اللهُ
وَحْدَهُ، لَا إِلَهَ إِلَّا اللهُ وَحْدَهُ لَا شَرِيكَ لَهُ، لَا
إِلَهَ إِلَّا اللهُ لَهُ الْمُلْكُ وَلَهُ الْحَمْدُ، لَا إِلَهَ إِلَّا اللهُ
وَلَا حَوْلَ وَلَا قُوَّةَ إِلَّا بِاللهِ»

---

[1] Al-Bukhāri 7/10, Muslim 4/1893.

[2] Al-Bukhāri, cf. Al-Asqalāni, *Fathul-Bāri* 8/ 144. The *Hadith* also mention him using the *Siwāk* (tooth stick).

152. *Laa 'ilaaha 'illallaahu wallaahu 'Akbar, laa 'ilaaha 'illallaahu wahdahu, laa 'ilaaha 'illallaahu wahdahu laa shareeka lahu, laa 'ilaaha 'illallaahu lahul-mulku wa lahul-hamdu, laa 'ilaaha 'illallaahu wa laa hawla wa laa quwwata 'illaa billaah.*

There is none worthy of worship but Allāh, Allāh is the Most Great. None has the right to be worshipped but Allāh alone. None has the right to be worshipped but Allāh alone, Who has no partner. There is none worthy of worship but Allāh, His is the dominion and His is the praise. There is none worthy of worship but Allāh, there is no power and no might but by Allāh.[1]

52. What to encourage the dying person to say

153. Whoever dies with the last words:

«لَا إِلَهَ إِلَّا اللهُ»

---

[1] At-Tirmithī and Ibn Mājah. See also Al-Albāni, *Sahih At-Tirmithī* 3/152 and *Sahih Ibn Mājah* 2/317.

Laa 'ilaaha 'illallaahu.

"There is none worthy of worship but Allāh," will enter Paradise.[1]

53. Invocation for when tragedy strikes

١٥٤-«إِنَّا للهِ وَإِنَّا إِلَيْهِ رَاجِعُونَ اللَّهُمَّ أُجُرْنِي فِي مُصِيبَتِي وَأَخْلِفْ لِي خَيْرًا مِنْهَا».

154. *'Innaa lillaahi wa 'innaa 'ilayhi raaji'oon, Allaahumma'-jurni fee museebatee wa 'akhlif lee khayran minhaa.*

We are from Allāh and unto Him we return. O Allāh take me out of my plight and bring to me after it something better.[2]

54. Invocation for closing the eyes of the dead

١٥٥-«اللَّهُمَّ اغْفِرْ لِفُلَانٍ (بِاسْمِهِ) وَارْفَعْ

---

[1] Abu Dawud 3/190. See also Al-Albāni, *Sahihul-Jāmi' As-Saghir* 5/432.

[2] Muslim 2/632.

دَرَجَتَهُ فِي الْمَهْدِيِّينَ، وَاخْلُفْهُ فِي عَقِبِهِ فِي
الْغَابِرِينَ، وَاغْفِرْ لَنَا وَلَهُ يَا رَبَّ الْعَالَمِينَ،
وَافْسَحْ لَهُ فِي قَبْرِهِ وَنَوِّرْ لَهُ فِيهِ».

155. *Allaahummaghfir li* (name of the person) *warfa' darajatahu fil-mahdiyyeena, wakhlufhu fee 'aqibihi fil-ghaabireena, waghfir-lanaa wa lahu yaa Rabbal-'aalameena, wafsah lahu fee qabrihi wa nawwir lahu feehi.*

O Allāh, forgive [*name of the person*] and elevate his station among those who are guided. Send him along the path of those who came before, and forgive us and him, O Lord of the worlds. Enlarge for him his grave and shed light upon him in it.[1]

55. Invocations for the dead in the Funeral prayer

١٥٦ـ«اللَّهُمَّ اغْفِرْ لَهُ وَارْحَمْهُ، وَعَافِهِ،
وَاعْفُ عَنْهُ، وَأَكْرِمْ نُزُلَهُ، وَوَسِّعْ مُدْخَلَهُ،

---

[1] Muslim 2/634.

وَاغْسِلْهُ بِالْمَاءِ وَالثَّلْجِ وَالْبَرَدِ، وَنَقِّهِ مِنَ
الْخَطَايَا كَمَا نَقَّيْتَ الثَّوْبَ الْأَبْيَضَ مِنَ
الدَّنَسِ، وَأَبْدِلْهُ دَارًا خَيْرًا مِنْ دَارِهِ، وَأَهْلًا
خَيْرًا مِنْ أَهْلِهِ، وَزَوْجًا خَيْرًا مِنْ زَوْجِهِ،
وَأَدْخِلْهُ الْجَنَّةَ، وَأَعِذْهُ مِنْ عَذَابِ الْقَبْرِ
[وَعَذَابِ النَّارِ]».

156. *Allaahum-maghfir lahu warhamhu, wa
'aafihi, wa'fu 'anhu, wa 'akrim nuzulahu, wa
wassi' mudkhalahu, waghsilhu bilmaa'i
waththalji walbaradi, wa naqqihi minal-
khataayaa kamaa naqqaytath-thawbal-
'abyadha minad-danasi, wa 'abdilhu daaran
khayran min daarihi, wa 'ahlan khayran min
'ahlihi, wa zawjan khayran min zawjihi, wa
'adkhilhul-jannata, wa 'a'ithhu min 'athaabil-
qabri [wa 'athaabin-naar].*

O Allāh, forgive him and have mercy on
him and give him strength and pardon
him. Be generous to him and cause his
entrance to be wide and wash him with

water and snow and hail. Cleanse him of his transgressions as white cloth is cleansed of stains. Give him an abode better than his home, and a family better than his family and a wife better than his wife. Take him into Paradise and protect him from the punishment of the grave [and from the punishment of Hell-fire].[1]

١٥٧ - «اللّٰهُمَّ اغْفِرْ لِحَيِّنَا، وَمَيِّتِنَا، وَشَاهِدِنَا، وَغَائِبِنَا، وَصَغِيرِنَا وَكَبِيرِنَا، وَذَكَرِنَا وَأُنْثَانَا. اللّٰهُمَّ مَنْ أَحْيَيْتَهُ مِنَّا فَأَحْيِهِ عَلَى الْإِسْلَام، وَمَنْ تَوَفَّيْتَهُ مِنَّا فَتَوَفَّهُ عَلَى الْإِيمَانِ، اللّٰهُمَّ لَا تَحْرِمْنَا أَجْرَهُ وَلَا تُضِلَّنَا بَعْدَهُ».

157. *Allaahum-maghfir lihayyinaa, wa mayyitinaa, wa shaahidinaa, wa ghaa'ibinaa, wa sagheerinaa wa kabeerinaa, wa thakarinaa wa 'unthaanaa. Allaahumma man 'ahyaytahu minnaa fa'ahyihi 'alal-'Islaami, wa man tawaffaytahu minnaa fatawaffahu 'alal-*

---

[1] Muslim 2/663.

'eemaani, Allaahumma laa tahrimnaa 'ajrahu wa laa tudhillanaa ba'dahu.

O Allāh forgive our living and our dead, those who are with us and those who are absent, our young and our old, our menfolk and our womenfolk. O Allāh, whomever you give life from among us give him life in Islam, and whomever you take way from us take him away in Faith. O Allāh, do not forbid us their reward and do not send us astray after them.[1]

١٥٨-«اللَّهُمَّ إِنَّ فُلاَنَ بْنَ فُلاَنٍ فِي ذِمَّتِكَ، وَحَبْلِ جِوَارِكَ، فَقِهِ مِنْ فِتْنَةِ الْقَبْرِ وَعَذَابِ النَّارِ، وَأَنْتَ أَهْلُ الْوَفَاءِ وَالْحَقِّ. فَاغْفِرْ لَهُ وَارْحَمْهُ إِنَّكَ أَنْتَ الْغَفُورُ الرَّحِيمُ».

158. *Allaahumma 'inna* [name the person] *fee thimmatika, wa habli jiwaarika, faqihi min fitnatil-qabri wa 'athaabin-naari, wa 'Anta 'ahlul-wafaa'i walhaqqi. Faghfir lahu*

---

[1] Ibn Mājah 1/480, Ahmad 2/368. See also Al-Albānī, *Sahih Ibn Mājah* 1/251.

166

warhamhu 'innaka 'Antal-Ghafoorur-Raheem.

O Allāh, surely [*name the person*] is under Your protection, and in the rope of Your security, so save him from the trial of the grave and from the punishment of the Fire. You fulfill promises and grant rights, so forgive him and have mercy on him. Surely You are Most Forgiving, Most Merciful.[1]

١٥٩-«اللَّهُمَّ عَبْدُكَ وَابْنُ أَمَتِكَ احْتَاجَ إِلَى رَحْمَتِكَ، وَأَنْتَ غَنِيٌّ عَنْ عَذَابِهِ، إِنْ كَانَ مُحْسِنًا فَزِدْ فِي حَسَنَاتِهِ، وَإِنْ كَانَ مُسِيئًا فَتَجَاوَزْ عَنْهُ».

159. *Allaahumma 'abduka wabnu 'amatika ihtaaja 'ilaa rahmatika, wa 'Anta ghaniyyun 'an 'athaabihi, 'in kaana muhsinan fazid fee hasanaatihi, wa 'in kaana musee'an fatajaawaz 'anhu.*

---

[1] Ibn Mājah, Abu Dawud 3/211. See also Al Albāni, *Sahih Ibn Mājah* 1/251.

O Allāh, Your male slave and the child of Your female slave is in need of Your mercy, and You are not in need of his torment. If he was pious then increase his rewards and if he was a transgressor then pardon him.[1]

56. Invocations for a child in the Funeral prayer

١٦٠-«اللَّهُمَّ أَعِذْهُ مِنْ عَذَابِ الْقَبْرِ» وَإِنْ قَالَ: «اللَّهُمَّ اجْعَلْهُ فَرَطًا وَذُخْرًا لِوَالِدَيْهِ، وَشَفِيعًا مُجَابًا. اللَّهُمَّ ثَقِّلْ بِهِ مَوَازِينَهُمَا وَأَعْظِمْ بِهِ أُجُورَهُمَا، وَأَلْحِقْهُ بِصَالِحِ الْمُؤْمِنِينَ، وَاجْعَلْهُ فِي كَفَالَةِ إِبْرَاهِيمَ، وَقِهِ بِرَحْمَتِكَ عَذَابَ الْجَحِيمِ، وَأَبْدِلْهُ دَارًا خَيْرًا مِنْ دَارِهِ، وَأَهْلًا خَيْرًا مِنْ أَهْلِهِ، اللَّهُمَّ اغْفِرْ لِأَسْلَافِنَا، وَأَفْرَاطِنَا، وَمَنْ سَبَقَنَا بِالْإِيمَانِ».

---

[1] Al-Hākim 1/359 who graded it authentic and Ath-Thahabi agreed with him. See also Al-Albāni, *Ahkāmul-Janā'iz*, p. 125.

160. *Allaahumma 'a'ith-hu min 'athaabil-qabri.* [or say:] *Allaahum-maj'alhu faratan wa thukhran liwaalidayhi, wa shafee'an mujaaban. Allaahumma thaqqil bihi mawaazeenahumaa wa 'a'dhim bihi 'ujoorahumaa, wa 'alhiqhu bisaalihil-mu'mineena, waj'alhu fee kafaalati 'Ibraaheema, wa qihi birahmatika 'athaabal-jaheemi, wa 'abdilhu daaran khayran min daarihi, wa 'ahlan khayran min 'ahlihi, Allaahum-maghfir li'aslaafinaa, wa 'afraatinaa wa man sabaqanaa bil'eemaan.*

O Allāh, protect him from the torment of the grave. [*It is also good to say:*] O Allāh, make him a precursor, a forerunner and a treasure for his parents and an answered intercessor. O Allāh, make him weigh heavily in their scales (of good) and magnify their reward. Make him join the righteous of the believers. Place him in the care of Ibrahim. Save him by Your mercy from the torment of Hell. Give him a home better than his home and a family better than his family. O Allāh, forgive

169

those who have gone (i.e. passed away) before us, our children lost (by death), and those who have preceded us in Faith.[1]

١٦١-«اللّٰهُمَّ اجْعَلْهُ لَنَا فَرَطًا، وَسَلَفًا، وَأَجْرًا».

161. *Allaahum-maj'alhu lanaa faratan, wa salafan, wa 'ajran.*

O Allāh, make him for us a precursor, a forerunner and a cause of reward.[2]

57. Invocation for the bereaved

١٦٢-«إِنَّ لِلّٰهِ مَا أَخَذَ، وَلَهُ مَا أَعْطَى وَكُلُّ شَيْءٍ عِنْدَهُ بِأَجَلٍ مُسَمَّى... فَلْتَصْبِرْ وَلْتَحْتَسِبْ».

162. *'Inna lillaahi maa 'akhadha, wa lahu maa*

[1] Ibn Qudāmah, *Al-Mughni* 3/416 and *Ad-Duroosul-Muhimmah li-'Aammatil-'Ummah*, pg. 15, by Shaikh 'Abdul-'Azīz bin Bāz.
[2] Al-Hasan (Al-Basri) used to recite *Surat Al-Fātihah* for a child's funeral and then say. Al-Bukhāri, *Kitābul-Janā'iz*, p. 65.

'a'taa, wa kullu shay'in 'indahu bi'ajalin musamman ... faltasbir waltahtasib.

Surely, Allāh takes what is His, and what He gives is His, and to all things He has appointed a time ... so have patience and be rewarded.[1]

It is also good to say:

«أَعْظَمَ اللهُ أَجْرَكَ، وَأَحْسَنَ عَزَاءَكَ وَغَفَرَ لِمَيِّتِكَ».

'A'dhamallaahu 'ajraka, wa 'ahsana 'azaa'aka wa ghafara limayyitika.

May Allāh magnify your reward, and make perfect your bereavement, and forgive your departed.[2]

58. Invocation to be recited when placing the dead in his grave

١٦٣ - «بِسْمِ اللهِ وَعَلَى سُنَّةِ رَسُولِ اللهِ».

163. *Bismillaahi wa 'alaa sunnati Rasoolillaahi.*

With the Name of Allāh and according to

---

[1] Al-Bukhāri 2/80, Muslim 2/636.

[2] An-Nawawi, *Kitābul-'Athkār*, p.126.

the *Sunnah* of the Messenger of Allāh.[1]

59. Invocation to be recited after burying the dead

١٦٤-«اللّٰهُمَّ اغْفِرْ لَهُ اللّٰهُمَّ ثَبِّتْهُ».

164. *Allaahum-maghfir lahu Allaahumma thabbithu.*

O Allāh, forgive him. O Allāh, strengthen him.[2]

60. Invocation for visiting the graves

١٦٥-«السَّلامُ عَلَيْكُمْ أَهْلَ الدِّيَارِ، مِنَ

[1] Abu Dawud 3/314 with an authentic chain. Ahmad also recorded it with the wording: With the Name of Allāh, and according to the religion of the Messenger of Allāh. Its chain is also authentic.

[2] The Prophet ﷺ used to stop after burying the dead and say to the people: "Ask Allāh to forgive your brother and pray for him to be strengthened, for indeed he is now being questioned." Abu Dawud 3/315, and Al-Hākim 1/370 who graded it authentic and Ath-Thahabi agreed.

الْمُؤْمِنِينَ وَالْمُسْلِمِينَ، وَإِنَّا إِنْ شَاءَ اللهُ بِكُمْ لَاحِقُونَ [وَيَرْحَمُ اللهُ الْمُسْتَقْدِمِينَ مِنَّا وَالْمُسْتَأْخِرِينَ] أَسْأَلُ اللهَ لَنَا وَلَكُمُ الْعَافِيَةَ».

165. *Assalaamu 'alaykum 'ahlad-diyaari, minal-mu'mineena walmuslimeena, wa 'innaa 'in shaa' Allaahu bikum laahiqoona, [wa yarhamullaahul-mustaqdimeena minnaa walmusta'khireena] 'as'alullaaha lanaa wa lakumul-'aafiyata.*

Peace be upon you, people of this abode, from among the believers and those who are Muslims, and we, by the Will of Allāh, shall be joining you. [May Allāh have mercy on the first of us and the last of us] I ask Allāh to grant us and you strength.[1]

61. Invocations for when the wind blows

١٦٦ـ«اللَّهُمَّ إِنِّي أَسْأَلُكَ خَيْرَهَا، وَأَعُوذُ بِكَ مِنْ شَرِّهَا».

---

[1] Muslim 2/671, Ibn Mājah 1/494, the portion in brackets is from Muslim 2/671.

166. *Allaahumma 'innee 'as'aluka khayrahaa, wa 'a'oothu bika min sharrihaa.*

O Allāh, I ask You for the good of it and seek refuge in You against its evil.[1]

١٦٧- «اللَّهُمَّ إِنِّي أَسْأَلُكَ خَيْرَهَا، وَخَيْرَ مَا فِيهَا، وَخَيْرَ مَا أُرْسِلَتْ بِهِ وَأَعُوذُ بِكَ مِنْ شَرِّهَا، وَشَرِّ مَا فِيهَا، وَشَرِّ مَا أُرْسِلَتْ بِهِ».

167. *Allaahumma 'innee 'as'aluka khayrahaa, wa khayra maa feehaa, wa khayra maa 'ursilat bihi wa a'oothu bika min sharrihaa, wa sharri maa feehaa, wa sharri maa 'ursilat bihi.*

O Allāh, I ask You for the good of it, for the good of what it contains, and for the good of what is sent with it. I seek refuge in You from the evil of it, from the evil of what it contains, and from the evil that is sent with it.[2]

---

[1] Abu Dawud 4/326, Ibn Mājah 2/1228. See also Al-Albāni, *Sahih Ibn Mājah* 2/305.
[2] Muslim 2/616, Al-Bukhāri 4/76.

62. Invocation for when it thunder

١٦٨- «سُبْحَانَ الَّذِي يُسَبِّحُ الرَّعْدُ بِحَمْدِهِ
وَالْمَلَائِكَةُ مِنْ خِيفَتِهِ».

168. Subhaanal-lathee yusabbihur-ra'du
bihamdihi walmalaa'ikatu min kheefatihi.

Glory is to Him Whom thunder and
angels glorify due to fear of Him.[1]

63. Some invocations for rain

١٦٩- «اللَّهُمَّ أَسْقِنَا غَيْثًا مُغِيثًا مَرِيئًا مَرِيعًا
نَافِعًا غَيْرَ ضَارٍّ، عَاجِلًا غَيْرَ آجِلٍ».

169. Allaahumma 'asqinaa ghaythan
mugheethan maree'an maree'an, naafi'an
ghayra dhaarrin, 'aajilan ghayra 'aajilin.

O Allāh, shower upon us abundant rain,

---

[1] Whenever Abdullah bin Zubair ﷺ would
hear thunder, he would abandon all
conversation and say this supplication. See *Al-
Muwatta'* 2/992. It was graded authentic by
Al-Albāni as a statement of Abdullah bin
Zubayr only.

beneficial not harmful, swiftly and not delayed.[1]

١٧٠ –«اللَّهُمَّ أَغِثْنَا، اللَّهُمَّ أَغِثْنَا، اللَّهُمَّ أَغِثْنَا».

170. *Allaahumma 'aghithnaa, Allaahumma 'aghithnaa, Allaahumma 'aghithnaa,*

O Allāh, send us rain. O Allāh, send us rain. O Allāh, send us rain.[2]

١٧١ –«اللَّهُمَّ اسْقِ عِبَادَكَ، وَبَهَائِمَكَ، وَانْشُرْ رَحْمَتَكَ، وَأَحْيِ بَلَدَكَ الْمَيِّتَ».

171. *Allaahum-masqi 'ibaadaka, wa bahaa'imaka, wanshur rahmataka, wa 'ahyi baladakal-mayyita.*

O Allāh, give water to Your slaves, and Your livestock, and spread Your mercy, and revive Your dead land.[3]

---

[1] Abu Dawud 1/303. See also Al-Albāni *Sahih Abu Dawud* 1/216.
[2] Al-Bukhāri 1/224, Muslim 2/613.
[3] Abu Dawud 1/305. Al-Albāni graded it good in *Sahih Abu Dawud* 1/218.

64. Invocation for when it rains

١٧٢-«اللَّهُمَّ صَيِّبًا نَافِعًا».

172. *Allaahumma sayyiban naafi'an.*

O Allāh, (bring) beneficial rain clouds.[1]

65. Supplication after it rains

١٧٣-«مُطِرْنَا بِفَضْلِ اللهِ وَرَحْمتِهِ».

173. *Mutirnaa bifadhlillaahi wa rahmatihi.*

It has rained by the bounty of Allāh and His mercy.[2]

66. Invocation for the withholding of the rain

١٧٤-«اللَّهُمَّ حَوَالَيْنَا وَلَا عَلَيْنَا. اللَّهُمَّ عَلَى الْأَكَامِ وَالظِّرَابِ، وَبُطُونِ الْأَوْدِيَةِ، وَمَنَابِتِ الشَّجَرِ».

174. *Allaahumma hawaalaynaa wa laa 'alaynaa. Allaahumma 'alal-'aakaami wadh-*

---

[1] Al-Bukhāri, cf. Al-Asqalāni, *Fathul-Bāri* 2/518.

[2] Al-Bukhāri 1/205, Muslim 1/83.

dhiraabi, wa butoonil-'awdiyati, wa manaabitish-shajari.

O Allāh, let it pass us and not fall upon us, but upon the hills and mountains, and the center of the valleys, and upon the forested lands.[1]

67. Invocation for sighting the new moon

١٧٥- «اللهُ أَكْبَرُ، اللَّهُمَّ أَهِلَّهُ عَلَيْنَا بِالأَمْنِ وَالإِيمَانِ، وَالسَّلَامَةِ وَالإِسْلَام، وَالتَّوْفِيقِ لِمَا تُحِبُّ رَبَّنَا وَتَرْضَى، رَبُّنَا وَرَبُّكَ اللهُ».

175. *Allaahu 'Akbar, Allaahumma 'ahillahu 'alayna bil'amni wal'eemaani, wassalaamati wal-'Islaami, wattawfeeqi limaa tuhibbu Rabbanaa wa tardhaa, Rabbunaa wa Rabbukallaahu.*

Allāh is the Most Great. O Allāh, bring us the new moon with security and Faith, with peace and in Islam, and in harmony

---

[1] Al-Bukhāri 1/224, Muslim 1/614.

with what our Lord loves and what pleases Him. Our Lord and your Lord is Allāh.[1]

68. Invocations for breaking the fast

١٧٦-«ذَهَبَ الظَّمَأُ وَابْتَلَّتِ الْعُرُوقُ، وَثَبَتَ الْأَجْرُ إِنْ شَاءَ اللهُ».

176. *Thahabadh-dhama'u wabtallatil-'urooqu, wa thabatal-'ajru 'in shaa' Allaah.*

The thirst is gone, the veins are moistened and the reward is confirmed, if Allāh wills.[2]

١٧٧-«اللَّهُمَّ إِنِّي أَسْأَلُكَ بِرَحْمَتِكَ الَّتِي وَسِعَتْ كُلَّ شَيْءٍ أَنْ تَغْفِرَ لِي».

177. *Allaahumma 'innee 'as'aluka birahmatikal-latee wasi'at kulla shay'in 'an taghfira lee.*

---

[1] At-Tirmithi 5/504, Ad-Darimi 1/336. See also Al-Albāni, *Sahih At-Tirmithi* 3/157.
[2] Abu Dawud 2/306 and others. See also Al-Albāni, *Sahihul-Jāmi' As-Saghir* 4/209.

O Allāh, I ask You by Your mercy, which encompasses all things, that You forgive me.[1]

69. Invocations before eating

178. When anyone of you begins eating, say:

«بِسْمِ اللهِ» .

Bismillaah.

With the Name of Allāh.

And if you forget then, when you remember, say:

«بِسْمِ اللهِ فِي أَوَّلِهِ وَآخِرِهِ» .

Bismillaahi fee 'awwalihi wa 'aakhirihi.

With the Name of Allāh, in the beginning and in the end.[2]

---

[1] Ibn Mājah 1/557 from a supplication of Abdullah bin 'Amr. Al-Hāfidh graded it as good in his checking of An-Nawawi's *Kitābul-'Athkār*. See *Sharhul-'Athkār* 4/342.

[2] Abu Dawud 3/347, At-Tirmithi 4/288. See Al-Albāni's *Sahih At-Tirmithi* 2/167.

179. Whomever Allāh has given food, should say:

«اللَّهُمَّ بَارِكْ لَنَا فِيهِ وَأَطْعِمْنَا خَيْرًا مِنْهُ».

Allaahumma baarik lanaa feehi wa 'at'imnaa khayran minhu.

O Allāh, bless us in it and provide us with better than it.

Whomever Allāh has given milk to drink, should say:

«اللَّهُمَّ بَارِكْ لَنَا فِيهِ وَزِدْنَا مِنْهُ».

Allaahumma baarik lanaa feehi wa zidnaa minhu.

O Allāh, bless us in it and give us more of it.[1]

70. Invocations after eating

١٨٠-«الْحَمْدُ للهِ الَّذِي أَطْعَمَنِي هَذَا، وَرَزَقَنِيهِ، مِنْ غَيْرِ حَوْلٍ مِنِّي وَلَا قُوَّةٍ».

---

[1] At-Tirmithi 5/506. See also Al-Albāni, *Sahih At-Tirmithi* 3/158.

180. *Alhamdu lillaahil-lathee 'at'amanee haathaa, wa razaqaneehi, min ghayri hawlin minnee wa laa quwwatin.*

Praise is to Allāh Who has given me this food and sustained me with it though I was unable to do it and powerless.[1]

١٨١-«الْحَمْدُ لِلهِ حَمْدًا كَثِيرًا طَيِّبًا مُبَارَكًا فِيهِ، غَيْرَ [مَكْفِيٍّ وَلَا] مُوَدَّعٍ، وَلَا مُسْتَغْنًى عَنْهُ رَبَّنَا».

181. *Alhamdu lillaahi hamdan katheeran tayyiban mubaarakan feehi, ghayra [makfiyyin wa laa] muwadda'in, wa laa mustaghnan 'anhu Rabbanaa.*

All praise is to Allāh, praise in abundance, good and blessed. It cannot [be compensated for, nor can it] be left, nor can it be done without, our Lord.[2]

---

[1] At-Tirmithi, Abu Dawud, and Ibn Mājah. See also Al-Albāni, *Sahih At-Tirmithi* 3/159.

[2] Al-Bukhāri 6/214, At-Tirmithi 5/507.

71. A dinner guest's invocation for his host

١٨٢-«اللَّهُمَّ بَارِكْ لَهُمْ فِيمَا رَزَقْتَهُمْ، وَاغْفِرْ لَهُمْ وَارْحَمْهُمْ».

182. *Allaahumma baarik lahum feemaa razaqtahum, waghfir lahum warhamhum.*

O Allāh, bless them in what You have provided for them, and forgive them and have mercy on them.[1]

72. Invocation for someone who gives you drink or offers it to you

١٨٣-«اللَّهُمَّ أَطْعِمْ مَنْ أَطْعَمَنِي وَاسْقِ مَنْ سَقَانِي».

183. *Allaahumma 'at'im man 'at'amanee wasqi man saqaanee.*

O Allāh, feed the one who has fed me and give drink to the one who has given me drink.[2]

---

[1] Muslim 3/1615.
[2] Muslim 3/126.

73. Invocation for a family who invites you to break your fast with them

١٨٤-«أَفْطَرَ عِنْدَكُمُ الصَّائِمُونَ، وَأَكَلَ طَعَامَكُمُ الْأَبْرَارُ، وَصَلَّتْ عَلَيْكُمُ الْمَلَائِكَةُ».

184. 'Aftara 'indakumus-saa'imoona, wa 'akala ta'aamakumul-'abraaru, wa sallat 'alaykumul-malaa'ikatu.

With you, those who are fasting have broken their fast, you have fed those who are righteous, and the angels recite their prayers upon you.[1]

74. Invocation for someone who offers you food when you are fasting, which you decline

185. When you are invited (to eat) then reply to the invitation. If you are fasting then invoke Allāh's blessings (on your

---

[1] Abu Dawud 3/367, Ibn Mājah 1/556, An-Nasā'i, *'Amalul-Yawm wal-Laylah* 296-8. Al-Albāni graded it authentic in *Sahih Abu Dawud* 2/730.

host), and if you are not fasting then eat.[1]

75. What to say when you are fasting and someone is rude to you

١٨٦ –«إِنِّي صَائِمٌ، إِنِّي صَائِمٌ» .

186. 'Innee saa'imun, 'innee saa'imun.

I am fasting. I am fasting.[2]

76. Invocation for when you see the first dates of the season

١٨٧ –«اللَّهُمَّ بَارِكْ لَنَا فِي ثَمَرِنَا، وَبَارِكْ لَنَا فِي مَدِينَتِنَا وَبَارِكْ لَنَا فِي صَاعِنَا، وَبَارِكْ لَنَا فِي مُدِّنَا» .

187. Allahumma baarik lanaa fee thamarinaa, wa baarik lanaa fee madeenatinaa wa baarik lanaa fee saa'inaa, wa baarik lanaa fee muddinaa.

O Allāh, bless us in our dates and bless us

---

[1] Muslim 2/1054.
[2] Al-Bukhāri, cf. Al-Asqalāni, Fathul-Bāri 4/103, Muslim 2/806.

in our town, bless us in our *Sā'* and in our *Mudd*.[1]

77. Invocation for sneezing

188. When you sneeze, then say:

«الْحَمْدُ لله».

Alhamdu lillaah.

All praises and thanks are to Allāh.

Your companion should say:

«يَرْحَمُكَ اللهُ».

Yarhamukallaah.

May Allāh have mercy upon you.

When someone says *Yarhamukallaah* to you then you should say:

«يَهْدِيكُمُ اللهُ وَيُصْلِحُ بَالَكُمْ».

Yahdeekumul-laahu wa yuslihu baalakum.

---

[1] Muslim 2/1000 (*Sā'* and *Mudd* are both dry measures used for agricultural produce by the Arabs in the Prophet's time. Of the two, the *Sā'* was the larger measure.) (Translator)

May Allāh guide you and set your affairs in order.[1]

78. What to say to the disbeliever if he sneezes and praises Allāh

١٨٩ - «يَهْدِيكُمُ اللهُ وَيُصْلِحُ بَالكُمْ».

189. *Yahdeekumullaahu wa yuslihu baalakum.*

May Allāh guide you and set your affairs in order.[2]

79. Invocation for the groom

١٩٠ - «بَارَكَ اللهُ لَكَ، وَبَارَكَ عَلَيْكَ؛ وَجَمَعَ بَيْنَكُمَا فِي خَيْرٍ».

190. *Baarakallaahu laka, wa baaraka 'alayka, wa jama'a baynakumaa fee khayrin.*

May Allāh bless you, and shower His blessings upon you, and join you together

---

[1] Al-Bukhāri 7/125.

[2] At-Tirmiṯhi 5/82, Ahmad 4/400, Abu Dawud 4/308. See also Al-Albāni, *Sahih At-Tirmiṯhi* 2/354.

in goodness.[1]

80. The groom's invocation and what he says upon purchasing an animal

When any of you marries a woman or purchases a maid-servant then let him say:

١٩١- «اللَّهُمَّ إِنِّي أَسْأَلُكَ خَيْرَهَا وَخَيْرَ مَا جَبَلْتَهَا عَلَيْهِ وَأَعُوذُ بِكَ مِنْ شَرِّهَا وَشَرِّ مَا جَبَلْتَهَا عَلَيْهِ».

191. *Allaahumma 'innee 'as'aluka khayrahaa wa khayra ma jabaltahaa 'alayhi wa 'a'oothu bika min sharrihaa wa sharri maa jabaltahaa 'alayhi.*

O Allāh, I ask You for the goodness of her and the goodness upon which You have created her, and I seek refuge in You from the evil of her and from the evil upon which You have created her.

If you purchase a camel then take hold of

---

[1] Abu Dawud, Ibn Mājah and At-Tirmithi. See also Al-Albāni, *Sahih At-Tirmithi* 1/316.

the top of its hump and say the same.[1]

81. Invocation to be recited before intercourse

١٩٢ -«بِسْمِ اللهِ. اللَّهُمَّ جَنِّبْنَا الشَّيْطَانَ،
وَجَنِّبِ الشَّيْطَانَ مَا رَزَقْتَنَا».

192. Bismillaah. Allaahumma jannibnash-Shaytaana, wa jannibish-Shaytaana maa razaqtanaa.

With the Name of Allāh. O Allāh, keep the Devil away from us and keep the Devil away from that which You provide for us.[2]

82. Invocation for anger

١٩٣ -«أَعُوذُ بِاللهِ مِنَ الشَّيْطَانِ الرَّجِيمِ».

193. ʾAʿoothu billaahi minash-Shaytaanir-rajeem.

I seek refuge in Allāh from Satan the

---

[1] Abu Dawud 2/248 and Ibn Mājah 1/617. See also Al-Albāni, Sahih Ibn Mājah 1/324.
[2] Al-Bukhāri 6/141, Muslim 2/1028.

outcast.[1]

83. What to say if you see someone afflicted by misfortune

١٩٤-«الْحَمْدُ للهِ الَّذِي عَافَانِي مِمَّا ابْتَلَاكَ بِهِ وَفَضَّلَنِي عَلَى كَثِيرٍ مِمَّنْ خَلَقَ تَفْضِيلًا».

194. Alhamdu lillaahil-lathee 'aafaanee mimmab-talaaka bihi wa fadhdhalanee 'alaa katheerin mimman khalaqa tafdheela.

Praise is to Allāh Who has spared me what He has afflicted you with, and preferred me greatly above much of what He has created.[2]

84. What to say while sitting in an assembly

Ibn Umar ﷺ said: Allāh's Messenger ﷺ used to repeat in a single sitting:

١٩٥-رَبِّ اغْفِرْ لِي وَتُبْ عَلَيَّ إِنَّكَ أَنْتَ

---

[1] Al-Bukhāri 7/99, Muslim 4/2015.
[2] At-Tirmithi 5/493,4. See also Al-Albāni, Sahih At-Tirmithi 3/153.

التَّوَّابُ الْغَفُورُ».

195. *Rabbighfir lee wa tub 'alayya 'innaka 'Antat-Tawwaabul-Ghafoor.*

My Lord, forgive me and accept my repentance, You are the Ever-Relenting, the All-Forgiving.[1]

85. The Expiation of Assembly – *Kaffāratul-Majlis*

١٩٦ -«سُبْحَانَكَ اللّٰهُمَّ وَبِحَمْدِكَ، أَشْهَدُ أَنْ لَا إِلٰهَ إِلَّا أَنْتَ، أَسْتَغْفِرُكَ وَأَتُوبُ إِلَيْكَ».

196. *Subhaanaka Allaahumma wa bihamdika, 'ash-hadu 'an laa 'ilaaha 'illaa 'Anta, 'astaghfiruka wa 'atoobu 'ilayka.*

Glory is to You, O Allāh, and praise is to You. I bear witness that there is none worthy of worship but You. I seek Your forgiveness and repent to You.[2]

---

[1] *Sahih Ibn Mājah* 2/321. See also Al-Albāni, *Sahih At-Tirmithi* 3/153.

[2] Abu Dawud, Ibn Mājah, At-Tirmithi and

86. Invocation for someone who says: "May Allāh forgive you"

١٩٧ – «وَلَكَ» .

197. *Wa laka.*

And you.[1]

87. Invocation for someone who does good to you

١٩٨ – «جَزَاكَ اللهُ خَيْرًا» .

198. *Jazaakallaahu khayran.*

An-Nasā'i. See also Al-Albāni, *Sahih At-Tirmithi* 3/153. Aishah 🌸 said: "Allāh's Messenger 🌟 did not sit in a gathering, and did not recite the Qur'ān, and did not perform any prayer without concluding by saying ... (then she quoted the above)." This was reported by An-Nasā'i in '*Amalul-Yawm wal-Laylah* (no. 308), and Dr. Farooq Hamādah graded it authentic in his checking of the same book, p. 273. See also Ahmad 6/77.

[1] Ahmad 5/82, and An-Nasā'i in '*Amalul-Yawm wal-Laylah* p. 218, with checking by Dr. Farooq Hamādah.

May Allāh reward you with good.[1]

88. Invocation for Allāh's protection from the False Messiah

199. Whoever memorizes ten *'Āyāt* (Verses) from the beginning of *Surat Al-Kahf*, will be protected from the False Messiah[2] if he recites them in every prayer after the final *Tashahhud* before ending the prayer, seeking the protection of Allāh from the trials of the False Messiah.[3]

89. Invocation for someone who tells you: "I love you for the sake of Allāh"

٢٠٠-«أَحَبَّكَ الَّذِي أَحْبَبْتَنِي لَهُ»

200. *'Ahabbakal-lathee 'ahbabtanee lahu.*

---

[1] At-Tirmithi (no. 2035). See also Al-Albāni, *Sahih At-Tirmithi* 2/200 and *Sahihul-Jāmi'* (no. 6244).
[2] Muslim 1/555, another version mentions the last ten *'Āyāt*, Muslim 1/556.
[3] See invocations no. 55 and 56 of this book.

May He for Whose sake you love me, love you.[1]

90. Invocation for someone who offers you a share of his wealth

٢٠١-«بَارَكَ اللهُ لَكَ فِي أَهْلِكَ وَمَالِكَ».

201. *Baarakallaahu laka fee 'ahlika wa maalika.*

May Allāh bless you in your family and your property.[2]

91. Invocation (upon receipt of the loan) for someone who lends you money

٢٠٢-«بَارَكَ اللهُ لَكَ فِي أَهْلِكَ وَمَالِكَ، إِنَّمَا جَزَاءُ السَّلَفِ الْحَمْدُ وَالْأَدَاءُ».

202. *Baarakallaahu laka fee 'ahlika wa maalika, 'innamaa jazaa'us-salafil-hamdu wal'adaa'.*

May Allāh bless you in your family and

---

[1] Abu Dawud 4/333. Al-Albāni graded it good in *Sahih Abu Dawud* 3/965.

[2] Al-Bukhāri, cf. Al-Asqalāni, *Fathul-Bāri* 4/88.

your wealth, surely the reward for a loan is praise and returning (what was borrowed).[1]

92. Invocation for fear of *Shirk*

٢٠٣-«اللَّهُمَّ إِنِّي أَعُوذُ بِكَ أَنْ أُشْرِكَ بِكَ وَأَنَا أَعْلَمُ، وَأَسْتَغْفِرُكَ لِمَا لَا أَعْلَمُ».

203. *Allaahumma 'innee 'a'oothu bika 'an 'ushrika bika wa 'anaa 'a'lamu, wa 'astaghfiruka limaa laa 'a'lamu.*

O Allāh, I seek refuge in You lest I associate anything with You knowingly, and I seek Your forgiveness for what I know not.[2]

93. Invocation for someone who tells you: "May Allāh bless you."

٢٠٤-«وَفِيكَ بَارَكَ اللهُ».

---

[1] An-Nasā'i, *'Amalul-Yawm wal-Laylah* p. 300, Ibn Mājah 2/809. See also Al-Albāni, *Sahih Ibn Mājah* 2/55.

[2] Ahmad 4/403. See also Al-Albāni, *Sahihul-Jāmi' As-Saghir* 3/233 and *Sahihut-Targhīb wat-Tarhīb* 1/19.

204. *Wa feeka baarakallaahu.*

And may Allāh bless you.[1]

94. Invocation against evil portent

٢٠٥-«اللَّهُمَّ لَا طَيْرَ إِلَّا طَيْرُكَ، وَلَا خَيْرَ إِلَّا
خَيْرُكَ، وَلَا إِلَهَ غَيْرُكَ».

205. *Allaahumma laa tayra 'illaa tayruka, wa laa khayra 'illaa khayruka, wa laa 'ilaaha ghayruka.*

O Allāh there is no portent other than Your portent, no goodness other than Your goodness, and none worthy of worship other than You.[2]

---

[1] Ibn As-Sunni, p. 138, (no. 278). See also Ibn Al-Qayyim, *Al-Wābil As-Sayyib*, p. 304, with checking by Basheer Muhammad ‘Uyoon.

[2] Ahmad 2/220, Ibn As-Sunni (no. 292). See also Al-Albāni, *Silsilatul-'Ahādīth As-Sahīhah* 3/54, (no. 1065). As for bodings of good, these used to please the Prophet ﷺ and so when he heard good words from someone, he used to say: "We have taken from you a good portent from your mouth," Abu Dawud, Ahmad. See

95. Invocation for riding in a vehicle or on an animal

٢٠٦- بِسْمِ اللهِ، الْحَمْدُ للهِ ﴿سُبْحَانَ ٱلَّذِى سَخَّرَ لَنَا هَٰذَا وَمَا كُنَّا لَهُ مُقْرِنِينَ ۝ وَإِنَّا إِلَىٰ رَبِّنَا لَمُنقَلِبُونَ﴾ الْحَمْدُ للهِ، الْحَمْدُ للهِ، الْحَمْدُ للهِ، اللهُ أَكْبَرُ، اللهُ أَكْبَرُ، اللهُ أَكْبَرُ، سُبْحَانَكَ اللَّهُمَّ إِنِّي ظَلَمْتُ نَفْسِي فَاغْفِرْ لِي، فَإِنَّهُ لَا يَغْفِرُ الذُّنُوبَ إِلَّا أَنْتَ».

206. *Bismillaah, Alhamdu lillaah. Subhaanal-lathee sakhkhara lanaa haathaa wa maa kunnaa lahu muqrineen. Wa 'innaa 'ilaa Rabbinaa lamunqaliboon. Alhamdu lillaah, alhamdu lillaah, alhamdu lillaah, Allaahu 'Akbar, Allaahu 'Akbar, Allaahu 'Akbar, subhaanakal-laahumma 'innee dhalamtu nafsee faghfir lee, fa'innahu laa yaghfiruth-thunooba 'illaa 'Anta.*

also Al-Albānī, *Silsilatul-'Ahādīth As-Sahīhah* 2/363, and it is with Abu Ash-Shaikh Al-Asfahāni in *'Akhlāqun-Nabiyy*, pg. 270.

With the Name of Allāh. Praise is to Allāh. Glory is to Him Who has provided this for us though we could never have had it by our efforts. Surely, unto our Lord we are returning. Praise is to Allāh. Praise is to Allāh. Praise is to Allāh. Allāh is the Most Great. Allāh is the Most Great. Allāh is the Most Great. Glory is to You. O Allāh, I have wronged my own soul. Forgive me, for surely none forgives sins but You.[1]

96. Invocation for traveling

٢٠٧- اللهُ أَكْبَرُ، اللهُ أَكْبَرُ، اللهُ أَكْبَرُ، ﴿سُبْحَٰنَ الَّذِى سَخَّرَ لَنَا هَٰذَا وَمَا كُنَّا لَهُۥ مُقْرِنِينَ ۝ وَإِنَّا إِلَىٰ رَبِّنَا لَمُنقَلِبُونَ﴾ اللَّهُمَّ إِنَّا نَسْأَلُكَ فِي سَفَرِنَا هَٰذَا الْبِرَّ وَالتَّقْوَى، وَمِنَ الْعَمَلِ مَا تَرْضَى، اللَّهُمَّ هَوِّنْ عَلَيْنَا سَفَرَنَا هَٰذَا وَاطْوِ عَنَّا بُعْدَهُ، اللَّهُمَّ أَنْتَ الصَّاحِبُ فِي السَّفَرِ، وَالْخَلِيفَةُ فِي

---

[1] Abu Dawud 3/34, At-Tirmithi 5/501. See also Al-Albāni, *Sahih At-Tirmithi* 3/156.

الْأَهْلِ، اللَّهُمَّ إِنِّي أَعُوذُ بِكَ مِنْ وَعْثَاءِ السَّفَرِ، وَكَآبَةِ الْمَنْظَرِ، وَسُوءِ الْمُنْقَلَبِ، فِي الْمَالِ وَالْأَهْلِ».

207. *Allaahu 'Akbar, Allaahu 'Akbar, Allaahu 'Akbar, Subhaanal-lathee sakhkhara lanaa haathaa wa maa kunnaa lahu muqrineen. Wa 'innaa 'ilaa Rabbinaa lamunqaliboon. Allaahumma 'innaa nas'aluka fee safarinaa haathal-birra wattaqwaa, wa minal-'amali maa tardhaa, Allaahumma hawwin 'alaynaa safaranaa haathaa watwi 'annaa bu'dahu, Allaahumma 'Antas-saahibu fis-safari, walkhaleefatu fil-'ahli, Allaahumma 'innee 'a'oothu bika min wa'thaa'is-safari, wa ka'aabatil-mandhari, wa soo'il-munqalabi fil-maali wal'ahli.*

Allāh is the Most Great. Allāh is the Most Great. Allāh is the Most Great. Glory is to Him Who has provided this for us though we could never have had it by our efforts. Surely, unto our Lord we are returning. O Allāh, we ask You on this our journey for goodness and piety, and for works that are pleasing to You. O Allāh, lighten this journey for us and make its distance easy for us. O Allāh, You are our Companion on the road and the One in Whose care we leave our family. O Allāh, I seek refuge in You from this journey's hardships, and from the wicked sights in store and from finding our family and property in misfortune upon returning.

(Upon returning recite the same again adding:)

«آيِبُونَ، تَائِبُونَ، عَابِدُونَ، لِرَبِّنَا حَامِدُونَ».

'Aa'iboona, taa'iboona, 'aabidoona, lirabbinaa haamidoon.

We return repentant to our Lord, worshipping our Lord, and praising our Lord.[1]

97. Invocation for entering a town or city

٢٠٨-«اللّهُمَّ رَبَّ السَّمٰوَاتِ السَّبْعِ وَمَا

[1] Muslim 2/978.

أَظْلَلْنَ، وَرَبَّ الْأَرَضِينَ السَّبْعِ وَمَا أَقْلَلْنَ،
وَرَبَّ الشَّيَاطِينِ وَمَا أَضْلَلْنَ، وَرَبَّ الرِّيَاحِ وَمَا
ذَرَيْنَ. أَسْأَلُكَ خَيْرَ هَذِهِ الْقَرْيَةِ وَخَيْرَ أَهْلِهَا،
وَخَيْرَ مَا فِيهَا، وَأَعُوذُ بِكَ مِنْ شَرِّهَا، وَشَرِّ
أَهْلِهَا، وَشَرِّ مَا فِيهَا».

208. *Allaahumma Rabbas-samaawaatis-sab'i
wa maa 'adhlalna, wa Rabbal-'aradheenas-
sab'i wa maa 'aqlalna, wa Rabbash-
shayaateeni wa maa 'adhlalna, wa Rabbar-
riyaahi wa maa tharayna. 'As'aluka khayra
haathihil-qaryati wa khayra 'ahlihaa, wa
khayra maa feehaa, wa 'a'oothu bika min
sharrihaa, wa sharri 'ahlihaa, wa sharri maa
feehaa.*

O Allāh, Lord of the seven heavens and
all they overshadow, Lord of the seven
worlds and all they uphold, Lord of the
devils and all they lead astray, Lord of the
winds and all they scatter. I ask You for
the goodness of this town and for the

goodness of its people, and for the goodness it contains. I seek refuge in You from its evil, from the evil of its people and from the evil it contains.[1]

98. Invocation for entering a market

٢٠٩-«لَا إِلَهَ إِلَّا اللهُ وَحْدَهُ لَا شَرِيكَ لَهُ، لَهُ الْمُلْكُ وَلَهُ الْحَمْدُ يُحْيِي وَيُمِيتُ وَهُوَ حَيٌّ لَا يَمُوتُ، بِيَدِهِ الْخَيْرُ، وَهُوَ عَلَى كُلِّ شَيْءٍ قَدِيرٌ».

209. Laa 'ilaaha 'illallaahu wahdahu laa shareeka lahu, lahul-mulku wa lahul-hamdu, yuhyee wa yumeetu, wa Huwa hayyun laa yamootu, biyadihil-khayru, wa Huwa 'alaa kulli shay'in Qadeer.

None has the right to be worshipped but Allāh alone, Who has no partner. His is

---

[1] Al-Hākim who graded it authentic and Ath-Thahabi agreed 2/100, and Ibn As-Sunni (no. 524). Al-Hāfidh graded it good in his checking of Al-'Athkār 5/154. Ibn Bāz said in Tuhfatul-'Akhyār p. 37, that An-Nasā'i recorded it with a good chain of narration.

the dominion and His is the praise. He brings life and He causes death, and He is living and does not die. In His Hand is all good, and He is Able to do all things.[1]

99. Invocation for when your vehicle or mount begins to fail

٢١٠-«بِسْمِ اللهِ».

210. *Bismillaahi*

With the Name of Allāh.[2]

100. The traveler's invocation for the one he leaves behind

٢١١-«أَسْتَوْدِعُكُمُ اللهَ الَّذِي لَا تَضِيعُ وَدَائِعُهُ».

211. *'Astawdi'ukumul-laahal-lathee laa tadhee'u wadaa'i'uhu.*

I leave you in the care of Allāh, as nothing

---

[1] At-Tirmithi 5/291, and Al-Hākim 1/538. Al-Albāni graded it good in *Sahih Ibn Mājah* 2/ 21 and *Sahih At-Tirmithi* 3/152.
[2] Abu Dawud 4/296. Al-Albāni graded it authentic in *Sahih Abu Dawud* 3/941.

is lost that is in His care.[1]

101. The resident's invocations for the traveler

٢١٢-«أَسْتَوْدِعُ اللهَ دِينَكَ، وَأَمَانَتَكَ، وَخَوَاتِيمَ عَمَلِكَ».

212. 'Astawdi'ullaaha deenaka, wa 'amaanataka, wa khawaateema 'amalika.

I leave your religion in the care of Allāh, as well as your safety, and the last of your deeds.[2]

٢١٣-«زَوَّدَكَ اللهُ التَّقْوَى، وَغَفَرَ ذَنْبَكَ، وَيَسَّرَ لَكَ الْخَيْرَ حَيْثُ مَا كُنْتَ».

213. Zawwadakal-laahut-taqwaa, wa ghafara thanbaka, wa yassara lakal-khayra haythu maa kunta.

May Allāh give you piety as your

---

[1] Ahmad 2/403, Ibn Mājah 2/943. See also Al-Albāni, Sahih Ibn Mājah 2/133.

[2] Ahmad 2/7, At-Tirmithi 5/499. See also Al-Albāni, Sahih At-Tirmithi 2/155.

provision, forgive your sins, and make goodness easy for you wherever you are.[1]

102. Glorifying and magnifying Allāh on the journey

214. Jabir ﷺ said: Whenever we went up a hill we would say Allaahu 'Akbar (Allāh is the Most Great) and when we descended we would say Subhaanallaah (Glory is to Allah).[2]

103. The traveler's invocation at dawn

٢١٥-«سَمِعَ سَامِعٌ بِحَمْدِ اللهِ، وَحُسْنِ بَلَائِهِ عَلَيْنَا. رَبَّنَا صَاحِبْنَا، وَأَفْضِلْ عَلَيْنَا عَائِذًا بِاللهِ مِنَ النَّارِ».

215. Sami'a saami'un bihamdillaahi wa husni

---

[1] At-Tirmiṭhi. See Al-Albāni, Sahih At-Tirmiṭhi, 3/155.

[2] Al-Bukhāri, cf. Al-Asqalāni, Fathul-Bāri 6/135.

balaa'ihi 'alaynaa. Rabbanaa saahibnaa, wa 'afdhil 'alaynaa 'aa'ithan billaahi minan-naar.

He Who listens has heard that we praise Allāh for the good things He gives us. Our Lord, be with us and bestow Your favor upon us. I seek the protection of Allāh from the Fire.[1]

---

[1] Muslim 4/2086, the meaning of *sami'a saami'un* (who listens has heard) is that 'a witness has witnessed our praise of Allāh due to His blessings and favor upon us.' It could also be read *samma'a saami'un*, in which case it means 'one who has heard this statement of mine will convey it to another and he will say it as well.' This is due to the attention given to the *Thikr* (remembrance of Allāh) and supplications made during the early morning hours. The meaning of his saying 'Our Lord, be with us and bestow Your favor upon us' is: 'Our Lord, protect us and guard us. Bless us with Your numerous bounties, and avert from us every evil.' See An-Nawawi, *Sharh Sahih Muslim* 17/39.

104. Invocation for a layover (stopping along the way) on the journey

٢١٦-«أَعُوذُ بِكَلِمَاتِ اللهِ التَّامَّاتِ مِنْ شَرِّ مَا خَلَقَ».

216. 'A'oothu bikalimaatil-laahit-taammaati min sharri maa khalaq.

I seek refuge in the Perfect Words of Allāh from the evil of what He has created.[1]

105. What to say upon returning from a journey

From every elevated point say Allaahu 'Akbar (Allāh is the Most Great) three times and then recite:

٢١٧-«لَا إِلَهَ إِلَّا اللهُ وَحْدَهُ لَا شَرِيكَ لَهُ، لَهُ الْمُلْكُ وَلَهُ الْحَمْدُ، وَهُوَ عَلَى كُلِّ شَيْءٍ قَدِيرٌ، آيِبُونَ، تَائِبُونَ، عَابِدُونَ، لِرَبِّنَا حَامِدُونَ، صَدَقَ اللهُ وَعْدَهُ، وَنَصَرَ عَبْدَهُ، وَهَزَمَ الْأَحْزَابَ وَحْدَهُ».

---

[1] Muslim 4/2080.

217. *Laa 'ilaaha 'illallaahu wahdahu laa shareeka lahu, lahul-mulku, wa lahul-hamdu, wa Huwa 'alaa kulli shay'in Qadeer, 'aa'iboona, taa'iboona, 'aabidoona, lirabbinaa haamidoona, sadaqallaahu wa'dahu, wa nasara 'abdahu, wa hazamal-'ahzaaba wahdahu.*

None has the right to be worshipped but Allāh alone, Who has no partner. His is the dominion and His is the praise, and He is Able to do all things. We return repentant to our Lord, worshipping our Lord, and praising our Lord. He fulfilled His Promise, He aided His slave, and He alone defeated the Confederates.[1]

106. What to say if something happens to please you or to displease you

When something happened that pleased him, the Prophet ﷺ used to say:

---

[1] Bukhārī 7/163, Muslim 2/980. The Prophet ﷺ used to say this when returning from a campaign or from *Hajj*.

٢١٨-«الْحَمْدُ لله الَّذِي بِنِعْمَتِهِ تَتِمُّ الصَّالِحَاتُ».

218. Alhamdu lillaahil-lathee bini'matihi tatimmus-saalihaat.

Praise is to Allāh Who by His blessings all good things are perfected.

And if something happened that displeased him, he used to say:

«الْحَمْدُ لله عَلَى كُلِّ حَالٍ».

Alhamdu lillaahi 'alaa kulli haal.

Praise is to Allāh in all circumstances.[1]

107. The excellence of asking for Allāh's blessings upon the Prophet ﷺ

219. The Prophet ﷺ said: "Whoever prays for Allāh's blessings upon me once, will be blessed for it by Allāh ten times."[2]

---

[1] Ibn As-Sunni, *'Amalul-Yawm wal-Laylah,* and Al-Hākim who graded it authentic 1/499. See also Al-Albāni, *Sahihul-Jāmi' As-Saghir* 4/201.
[2] Muslim 1/288.

220. The Prophet ﷺ said: "Do not make my grave a place of ritual celebration, but pray for Allāh's blessings upon me, for your blessings reach me from wherever you are."[1]

221. The Prophet ﷺ said: "The miser is the one in whose presence I am mentioned yet does not pray for Allāh's blessings upon me."[2]

222. The Prophet ﷺ said: "Indeed Allāh has angels who roam the earth and they convey to me the greetings (or prayers of peace) of my 'Ummah (nation)."[3]

223. The Prophet ﷺ said: "No one sends greetings (or prayers of peace) upon me but Allāh returns my soul to me so that I

---

[1] Abu Dawud 2/218, Ahmad 2/367. Al-Albāni graded it authentic in *Sahih Abu Dawud* 2/383.

[2] At-Tirmithi 5/551 and others. See also Al-Albāni, *Sahih At-Tirmithi* 3/177 and *Sahihul-Jāmi' As-Saghir* 3/25.

[3] An-Nasā'i, Al-Hākim 2/421. Al-Albāni graded it authentic in *Sahih An-Nasā'i* 1/274.

may return his greetings."[1]

108. Spreading the greetings of *Salām* (Peace)

224. The Prophet ﷺ said: "You shall not enter Paradise until you believe, and you have not believed until you love one another. Shall I tell you of something you can do to make you love one another? Spread the greetings of *Salām* (peace) amongst yourselves (i.e. between each other)."[2]

225. The Prophet ﷺ said: "There are three things which whoever gathers all of them together, then he has gathered *Imān* (Faith): justice with oneself, greeting people with greetings of *Salām* (peace), and freeing oneself from stinginess."[3]

---

[1] Abu Dawud (no. 2041). Al-Albāni graded it good in *Sahih Abu Dawud* 1/383.
[2] Muslim 1/74 and others.
[3] Al-Bukhāri, cf. Al-Asqalāni, *Fathul-Bāri* 1/82 as a statement of the Companion ʿAmmār ﷺ.

226. Abdullah bin 'Umar ﷺ said: A man asked the Prophet ﷺ, "What is the best act of Islām?" He said, "To feed others and to give greetings of *Salām* (peace) to those whom you know and to those whom you do not know."[1]

109. How to reply to a disbeliever if he says *Salām* to you

227. If one of the People of the Scripture (i.e. Christians and Jews) greets you saying *As-Salaamu 'alaykum,* then say (to him):

«وَعَلَيْكُمْ».

Wa 'alaykum.[2]

And upon you.

110. Invocation upon hearing the cock's crow or the bray of a donkey

228. When you hear the cock's crow, ask

---

[1] Al-Bukhāri, cf. Al-Asqalāni, *Fathul-Bāri* 1/55, Muslim 1/65.

[2] Al-Bukhāri, cf. Al-Asqalāni, *Fathul-Bāri* 11/42, Muslim 4/1705.

Allāh for His favor upon you for surely it has seen an angel. When you hear the bray of a donkey, seek refuge in Allāh from Satan, for surely it has seen a devil.[1]

111. Invocation upon hearing a dog barking in the night

229. When you hear a dog barking or a donkey braying in the night, then seek refuge in Allāh from them, for surely they have seen what you see not.[2]

112. Invocation for someone you have spoken ill to

٢٣٠-«اللَّهُمَّ فَأَيُّمَا مُؤْمِنٍ سَبَبْتُهُ فَاجْعَلْ ذَلِكَ لَهُ قُرْبَةً إِلَيْكَ يَوْمَ الْقِيَامَةِ»

230. *Allaahumma fa'ayyumaa mu'minin*

---

[1] Al-Bukhāri, cf. Al-Asqalāni, *Fathul-Bāri* 6/350, Muslim 4/2092.

[2] Abu Dawud 4/327, Ahmad 3/306. Al-Albāni graded it authentic in *Sahih Abu Dawud* 3/961.

sababtuhu faj'al thaalika lahu qurbatan 'ilayka yawmal-qiyaamati.

O Allāh, whomever of the believers I have abused, give him the reward of a sacrificial slaughter for it on the Day of Resurrection.[1]

113. How a Muslim should praise another Muslim

231. If any of you praises his companion then let him say:

«أَحْسِبُ فُلَانًا وَاللهُ حَسِيبُهُ».

'Ahsibu fulaanan wallaahu haseebuhu.

I consider (such and such a person), and Allāh is his Assessor,

«وَلَا أُزَكِّي عَلَى اللهِ أَحَدًا».

wa laa 'uzakkee 'alallaahi 'ahadan

(meaning: and I cannot claim anyone to

---

[1] Al-Bukhāri, cf. Al-Asqalāni, *Fathul-Bāri* 11/171, Muslim 4/2007. The wording in Muslim's report is: 'make it a purification for him and a source of mercy.'

be pious before Allāh) if you know of this (good character trait in the person) to be such and such (saying what he thinks is praiseworthy in that person).[1]

114. What a Muslim should say when he is praised

٢٣٢-«اللَّهُمَّ لَا تُؤَاخِذْنِي بِمَا يَقُولُونَ، وَاغْفِرْ لِي مَا لَا يَعْلَمُونَ [وَاجْعَلْنِي خَيْرًا مِمَّا يَظُنُّونَ]».

232. Allaahumma laa tu'aakhithnee bimaa yaqooloona, waghfir lee maa laa ya'lamoona [waj'alnee khayram-mimmaa yadhunnoon].

O Allāh, do not call me to account for what they say and forgive me for what they have no knowledge of [and make me better than they imagine].[2]

---

[1] Muslim 4/2296.

[2] Al-Bukhāri, Al-'Adabul-Mufrad no. 761. See Al-Albāni, Sahih Al-'Adabul-Mufrad (no. 585). The portion between brackets if from Al-Bayhaqi, Shu'ab Al-Imān 4/228, and comes another account.

115. The pilgrim's announcement of his arrival for *Hajj* or *'Umrah*

٢٣٣-«لَبَّيْكَ اللَّهُمَّ لَبَّيْكَ، لَبَّيْكَ لَا شَرِيكَ لَكَ لَبَّيْكَ، إِنَّ الْحَمْدَ، وَالنِّعْمَةَ، لَكَ وَالْمُلْكَ، لَا شَرِيكَ لَكَ».

233. *Labbayk Allaahumma labbayk, labbayk laa shareeka laka labbayk, 'innal-hamda, wanni'mata, laka walmulk, laa shareeka laka.*

I am here at Your service, O Allāh, I am here at Your service. I am here at Your service, You have no partner, I am here at Your service. Surely the praise, and blessings are Yours, and the dominion. You have no partner.[1]

116. Saying *Allāhu 'Akbar* when passing the Black Stone

234. The Prophet ﷺ performed *Tawāf* riding a camel. Every time he passed the corner (containing the Black Stone), he

---

[1] Al-Bukhāri, cf. Al-Asqalāni, *Fathul-Bāri* 3/ 408, Muslim 2/841.

would point to it with something that he was holding and say: *Allaahu 'Akbar* (Allāh is the Most Great)![1]

117. Invocation to be recited between the Yemenite Corner and the Black Stone

٢٣٥ - ﴿رَبَّنَآ ءَاتِنَا فِى ٱلدُّنْيَا حَسَنَةً وَفِى ٱلْأَخِرَةِ حَسَنَةً وَقِنَا عَذَابَ ٱلنَّارِ﴾

235. *Rabbanaa 'aatinaa fid-dunyaa hasanatan wa fil-'aakhirati hasanatan wa qinaa 'athaaban-naar.*

Our Lord, grant us the good things in this world and the good things in the next life and save us from the punishment of the Fire.[2]

---

[1] Al-Bukhāri, cf. Al-Asqalāni, *Fathul-Bāri* 3/ 476. See also 472. The 'something' that was referred to in this *Hadith* was a cane.

[2] Abu Dawud 2/179, Ahmad 3/411, Al-Baghawi, *Sharhus-Sunnah* 7/128. Al-Albāni graded it good in *Sahih Abu Dawud* 1/354. The *Ayat* is from *Surat Al-Baqarah*, 2:201.

118. Invocation to be recited while standing at Safa and Marwah

236. Whenever the Prophet ﷺ approached Mount Safa, he would recite:

«﴿إِنَّ ٱلصَّفَا وَٱلْمَرْوَةَ مِن شَعَآئِرِ ٱللَّهِ﴾ أَبْدَأُ بِمَا بَدَأَ اللَّهُ بِهِ».

'Innas-Safaa wal-Marwata min sha'aa'irillaah. 'Abda'u bimaa bada'allaahu bihi.

Surely Safa and Marwah are among the signs of Allāh. I begin by that which Allāh began.

He began (his *Sa'y*) at Mount Safa climbing it until he could see the House. He then faced the *Qiblah* repeating the words:

«لَا إِلَهَ إِلَّا اللهُ، اللهُ أَكْبَرُ».

Laa 'ilaaha 'illallaah, Allaahu 'Akbar

There is none worthy of worship but Allāh, and Allāh is the Most Great.

Then he said:

«لَا إِلَهَ إِلَّا اللهُ وَحْدَهُ لَا شَرِيكَ لَهُ، لَهُ الْمُلْكُ
وَلَهُ الْحَمْدُ، وَهُوَ عَلَى كُلِّ شَيْءٍ قَدِيرٌ، لَا إِلَهَ
إِلَّا اللهُ وَحْدَهُ، أَنْجَزَ وَعْدَهُ، وَنَصَرَ عَبْدَهُ،
وَهَزَمَ الْأَحْزَابَ وَحْدَهُ».

*Laa 'ilaaha 'illallaahu wahdahu laa shareeka
lahu, lahul-mulku wa lahul-hamdu wa Huwa
'alaa kulli shay'in Qadeer, laa 'ilaaha 'illallaahu
wahdahu, 'anjaza wa'dahu, wa nasara 'abdahu,
wa hazamal 'ahzaaba wahdahu.*

None has the right to be worshipped but
Allāh alone, Who has no partner, His is the
dominion and His is the praise, and He is
Able to do all things. None has the right to
be worshipped but Allāh alone, He
fulfilled His Promise, He aided His slave,
and He alone defeated Confederates.

Then he would ask Allāh for what he
liked, repeating the same thing like this
three times. He did at Mount Marwah as
he did at Mount Safa.[1]

---

[1] Muslim 2/888.

119. Invocation to be recited on the Day of Arafāt

The Prophet ﷺ said: The best invocation is that of the Day of Arafāt, and the best that anyone can say is what I and the Prophets before me have said:

٢٣٧-«لَا إِلٰهَ إِلَّا اللهُ وَحْدَهُ لَا شَرِيكَ لَهُ، لَهُ الْمُلْكُ وَلَهُ الْحَمْدُ، وَهُوَ عَلَى كُلِّ شَيْءٍ قَدِيرٌ».

237. *Laa 'ilaaha 'illallaahu wahdahu laa shareeka lahu, lahul-mulku wa lahul-hamdu wa Huwa 'alaa kulli shay'in Qadeer.*

None has the right to be worshipped but Allāh alone, Who has no partner. His is the dominion and His is the praise, and He is Able to do all things.[1]

120. Supplication to be recited at the sacred area of Muzdalifah

238. The Prophet ﷺ rode his camel, Al-Qaswā', until he reached the sacred area

---

[1] At-Tirmithi. Al-Albāni graded it good in *Sahih At-Tirmithi* 3/184, and also *Silsilatul-'Ahādīth As-Sahīhah* 4/6.

(Al-Mash'aril-Haraam). Then he faced the *Qiblah* and invoked Allāh, and repeatedly said the words: *Allaahu 'Akbar* (Allāh is the Most Great), *Allaahu 'Ahad* (Allāh is One) and *Laa 'ilaaha 'illallaah* (There is none worthy of worship but Allāh). He remained stationary until the sky became yellow with the dawn, and then pressed on before sunrise.[1]

121. Saying *Allāhu 'Akbar* while stoning the three pillars at Mina

239. The Prophet ﷺ said *Allaahu 'Akbar* (Allāh is the Most Great) with each pebble he threw at the three pillars. Then he went forward, stood facing the *Qiblah* and raised his hands and called upon Allāh. That was after (stoning) the first and second pillar. As for the third, he stoned it and called out *Allaahu 'Akbar* with every pebble he threw, but when he was finished he left without standing at it (for supplications).[2]

---

[1] Muslim 2/891.
[2] Al-Bukhāri, cf. Al-Asqalāni, *Fathul-Bāri* 3/581, 3, 4, and Muslim.

122. What to say when surprised or startled

٢٤٠-«سُبْحَانَ اللهِ».

240. *Subhaanallaah!*

   (Glory is to Allāh).[1]

٢٤١-«اللهُ أَكْبَرُ».

241. *Allaahu 'Akbar!*

   (Allāh is the Most Great).[2]

123. What to say when something that pleases you happens

242. Whenever something happened that pleased him or made him happy, the Prophet ﷺ used to prostrate himself in thanks to Allāh, the Blessed, the All-Mighty.[3]

---

[1] Al-Bukhāri, cf. Al-Asqalāni, *Fathul-Bāri* 1/ 210, 390, 414 and Muslim 4/1857.

[2] Al-Bukhāri, cf. Al-Asqalāni, *Fathul-Bāri* 8/ 441. See also Al-Albāni, *Sahih At-Tirmithi* 2/ 103, 235, Ahmad 5/218.

[3] Abu Dawud, Ibn Mājah, At-Tirmithi. See

124. What to say when you feel a pain in your body

243. Put your hand on the place where you feel pain and say:

«بِسْمِ اللهِ» .

Bismillaah.

With the Name of Allāh (three times).

Then say:

«أَعُوذُ بِاللهِ وَقُدْرَتِهِ مِنْ شَرِّ مَا أَجِدُ وَأُحَاذِرُ» .

'A'oothu billaahi wa qudratihi min sharri maa 'ajidu wa 'uhaathiru.

I seek refuge in Allāh and in His Power from the evil of what I find and of what I guard against.[1]

125. What to say when you fear you may afflict something with the evil eye

244. If you see anything of your brother

---

also Al-Albāni, *Sahih Ibn Mājah* 1/233, and *'Irwā'ul-Ghalīl* 2/226.

[1] Muslim 4/1728.

that pleases you, or of his person or of his property [then ask Allāh to bless him in it] for the envious eye is real.[1]

126. What to say when you feel frightened

٢٤٥-«لَا إِلَهَ إِلَّا اللهُ».

245. *Laa 'ilaaha 'illallaah!*

There is none worthy of worship but Allāh![2]

127. What to say when slaughtering or sacrificing an animal

٢٤٦-«بِسْمِ اللهِ وَاللهُ أَكْبَرُ [اللَّهُمَّ مِنْكَ وَلَكَ]
اللَّهُمَّ تَقَبَّلْ مِنِّي».

246. *Bismillaahi wallaahu 'Akbar*

---

[1] Ahmad 4/447, Ibn Mājah, Malik. Al-Albāni graded it authentic in *Sahihul-Jāmi' As-Saghir* 1/212. Also see Al-Arna'ut's checking of Ibn Al-Qayyim's *Zādul-Ma'ād* 4/170.

[2] Al-Bukhāri, cf. Al-Asqalāni, *Fathul-Bāri* 6/181, Muslim 4/2208.

[Allaahumma minka wa laka] Allaahumma taqabbal minnee.

With the Name of Allāh, Allah is the Most Great! [O Allāh, from You and to You.] O Allāh, accept it from me.[1]

128. What to say to foil the devil's plots

٢٤٧-أَعُوذُ بِكَلِمَاتِ اللهِ التَّامَّاتِ الَّتِي لَا يُجَاوِزُهُنَّ بَرٌّ وَلَا فَاجِرٌ مِنْ شَرِّ مَا خَلَقَ، وَبَرَأَ وَذَرَأَ، وَمِنْ شَرِّ مَا يَنْزِلُ مِنَ السَّمَاءِ، وَمِنْ شَرِّ مَا يَعْرُجُ فِيهَا، وَمِنْ شَرِّ مَا ذَرَأَ فِي الْأَرْضِ، وَمِنْ شَرِّ مَا يَخْرُجُ مِنْهَا، وَمِنْ شَرِّ فِتَنِ اللَّيْلِ وَالنَّهَارِ، وَمِنْ شَرِّ كُلِّ طَارِقٍ إِلَّا طَارِقًا يَطْرُقُ بِخَيْرٍ يَا رَحْمَنُ».

247. '*A'oothu bikalimaatil-laahit-taammaatil-latee laa yujaawizuhunna barrun wa laa faajirun min sharri maa khalaqa, wa bara'a*

---

[1] Muslim 3/1557, Al-Bayhaqi 9/287.

wa thara'a, wa min sharri maa yanzilu minas-samaa'i, wa min sharri maa ya'ruju feehaa, wa min sharri maa thara'a fil-'ardhi, wa min sharri ma yakhruju minhaa, wa min sharri fitanil-layli wannahaari, wa min sharri kulli taariqin 'illaa taariqan yatruqu bikhayrin yaa Rahmaan.

I seek refuge in the Perfect Words of Allāh – which neither the upright nor the corrupt may overcome – from the evil of what He created, of what He made, and of what He scattered, from the evil of what descends from the heavens, and of what rises up to them, from the evil of what He scattered in the earth and of what emerges from it, from the evil trials of night and day, and from the evil of every night visitor, except the night visitor who comes with good. O Merciful One.[1]

---

[1] Ahmad 3/419, with an authentic chain of narration, and Ibn As-Sunni (no. 637). Al-Arna'ut, graded its chain authentic in his checking of *Al-'Aqīdah At-Tahawīyyah* p. 133. See also *Majma'uz-Zawā'id*, 10/127.

129. Repentance and seeking forgiveness

248. Allāh's Messenger ﷺ said: "By Allāh, I seek the forgiveness of Allāh, and repent to Him more than seventy times in a day."[1]

249. Allāh's Messenger ﷺ said: "O people, repent to Allāh, for I verily repent to Him one hundred times a day."[2]

250. Allāh's Messenger ﷺ said: Whoever says:

«أَسْتَغْفِرُ اللهَ الْعَظِيمَ الَّذِي لَا إِلَهَ إِلَّا هُوَ الْحَيُّ الْقَيُّومُ وَأَتُوبُ إِلَيْهِ» .

'Astaghfirullaahal-'Adheemal-lathee laa 'ilaaha 'illaa Huwal-Hayyul-Qayyoomu wa 'atoobu 'ilayhi.

I seek the forgiveness of Allāh the Mighty, Whom there is none worthy of worship

---

[1] Al-Bukhāri, cf. Al-Asqalāni, *Fathul-Bāri* 11/101.

[2] Muslim 4/2076.

except Him, the Living, the Eternal, and I repent to Him,

Allāh will forgive him even if he has deserted the army's ranks.[1]

251. Allāh's Messenger ﷺ said: "The closest that the Lord comes to the slave is in the last portion of the night. So, if you are able to be among those who remember Allāh in this hour, then be among them."[2]

252. Allāh's Messenger ﷺ said: "The closest that the slave comes to his Lord is when he is prostrating, so invoke Allāh much (in prostration)."[3]

---

[1] Abu Dawud 2/85, At-Tirmithi 5/569, and Al-Hākim who declared it authentic and Ath-Thahabi agreed with him 1/511. Al-Albāni graded it authentic *in Sahih At-Tirmithi* 3/182. See also *Jāmi'ul-'Usool li-'Ahādith Ar-Rasool* 4/389-90 checked by Al-Arna'ut.

[2] At-Tirmithi, An-Nasā'i 1/279 and Al-Hākim. See also Al-Albāni, *Sahih At-Tirmithi* 3/183, and *Jāmi'ul-'Usool* with Al-Arna'ut's checking 4/144.

[3] Muslim 1/350.

253. Allāh's Messenger ﷺ said: "It is a heavy thing for my heart if I do not seek Allāh's forgiveness a hundred times a day."[1]

130. The excellence of remembering Allāh

254. Allāh's Messenger ﷺ said: Whoever says:

«سُبْحَانَ اللهِ وَبِحَمْدِهِ».

Subhaanallaahi wa bihamdihi.

Glorified is Allāh and praised is He,

one hundred times a day, will have his sins forgiven even if they are like the

---

[1] Muslim 4/2075. Ibn 'Athīr explains that the Prophet ﷺ was always vigilant in his remembrance and drawing near to Allāh, and if he forgot to do any of what he normally did from time to time, or it slipped his mind, he felt as if he had wronged himself and so he would begin to seek the forgiveness of Allāh. See *Jāmi'ul-'Usool* 4/386.

foam of the sea.[1]

255. Allāh's Messenger ﷺ said: Whoever says:

«لَا إِلَهَ إِلَّا اللهُ وَحْدَهُ لَا شَرِيكَ لَهُ، لَهُ الْمُلْكُ وَلَهُ الْحَمْدُ، وَهُوَ عَلَى كُلِّ شَيْءٍ قَدِيرٌ».

Laa 'ilaaha 'illallaahu wahdahu laa shareeka lahu, lahul-mulku wa lahul-hamdu wa Huwa 'alaa kulli shay'in Qadeer.

None has the right to be worshipped but Allāh alone, Who has no partner. His is the dominion and His is the praise, and He is Able to do all things,

ten times, will have the reward for freeing four slaves from the Children of Isma'il.[2]

256. Allāh's Messenger ﷺ said: Two words are light on the tongue, weigh heavily in the balance, and are loved by

---

[1] Al-Bukhāri 7/168, Muslim 4/2071, see also invocation no. 91 of this book.

[2] Al-Bukhāri 7/67, Muslim 4/2071, see also invocation no. 93 of this book.

the Most Merciful One:

«سُبْحَانَ اللهِ وَبِحَمْدِهِ سُبْحَانَ اللهِ الْعَظِيمِ» .

Subhaanal-laahi wa bihamdihi, Subhaanal-laahil-'Adheem.

Glorified is Allāh and praised is He, Glorified is Allāh the Most Great.[1]

257. Allāh's Messenger ﷺ said: For me to say:

«سُبْحَانَ اللهِ، وَالْحَمْدُ للهِ، وَلَا إِلَهَ إِلَّا اللهُ،
وَاللهُ أَكْبَرُ» .

Subhaanallaahi, walhamdu lillaahi, wa laa 'ilaaha 'illallaahu, wallaahu 'Akbar.

Glory is to Allāh, and praise is to Allāh, and there is none worthy of worship but Allāh, and Allāh is the Most Great.

is dearer to me than all that the sun rises upon (i.e. the whole world).[2]

258. Allāh's Messenger ﷺ said, "Is

---
[1] Al-Bukhāri 7/168, Muslim 4/2072.
[2] Muslim 4/2072.

anyone of you incapable of earning one thousand *Hasanah* (rewards) in a day?" Someone from his gathering asked, "How can anyone of us earn a thousand *Hasanah*?" He said, "Glorify Allāh a hundred times and a thousand *Hasanah* will be written for you, or a thousand sins will be wiped away."[1]

259. Whoever says:

«سُبْحَانَ اللهِ الْعَظِيمِ وَبِحَمْدِهِ» .

Subhaanallaahil-'Adheemi wa bihamdihi.

Glorified is Allāh the Most Great and praised is He,

will have a date palm planted for him in Paradise.[2]

260. Allāh's Messenger ﷺ said, "O Abdullah bin Qais, should I not point you

---

[1] Muslim 4/2073.

[2] At-Tirmithi 5/511, and Al-Hākim who graded it authentic and Ath-Thahabi agreed 1/501. See also Al-Albāni, *Sahihul-Jāmi' As-Saghir* 5/531 and *Sahih At-Tirmithi* 3/160.

to one of the treasures of Paradise?" I said, "Yes, O Messenger of Allāh." So he told me to say:

«لَا حَوْلَ وَلَا قُوَّةَ إِلَّا بِاللهِ».

Laa hawla wa laa quwwata 'illaa billaah.

There is no power and no might except by Allāh.[1]

261. Allāh's Messenger ﷺ said: The most beloved words to Allāh are four:

«سُبْحَانَ اللهِ».

Subhaanallaah.

Glorified is Allāh, and

«وَالْحَمْدُ لِلَّهِ».

Walhamdu lillaah.

The praise is for Allāh, and

«وَلَا إِلَهَ إِلَّا اللهُ».

Wa laa 'ilaaha 'illallaah.

[1] Al-Bukhāri, cf. Al-Asqalāni, *Fathul-Bāri* 11/213, Muslim 4/2076.

There is none worthy of worship but Allāh, and

«وَاللهُ أَكْبَرُ».

Wallaahu 'Akbar.

Allāh is the Most Great.

It does not matter which one you start by.[1]

262. A desert Arab came to Allāh's Messenger ﷺ and said, "Teach me a word that I can say." The Prophet told him to say:

«لَا إِلٰهَ إِلَّا اللهُ وَحْدَهُ لَا شَرِيكَ لَهُ، اللهُ أَكْبَرُ كَبِيرًا، وَالْحَمْدُ للهِ كَثِيرًا، سُبْحَانَ اللهِ رَبِّ الْعَالَمِينَ، لَا حَوْلَ وَلَا قُوَّةَ إِلَّا بِاللهِ الْعَزِيزِ الْحَكِيمِ».

Laa 'ilaaha 'illallaahu wahdahu laa shareeka lahu, Allaahu 'Akbaru kabeeran, walhamdu lillaahi katheeran, Subhaanallaahi Rabbil-

---

[1] Muslim 3/1685.

'aalameen, laa hawla wa laa quwwata 'illaa billaahil-'Azeezil-Hakeem.

There is none worthy of worship but Allāh, Who has no partner, Allāh is the Great, the Most Great, and praise is to Allāh in abundance, glory is to Allāh, Lord of the worlds. There is no power and no might but by Allāh the Mighty, the Wise.

He said, "That is for my Lord, but what about me?" The Prophet ﷺ told him to say:

«اللَّهُمَّ اغْفِرْ لِي، وَارْحَمْنِي، وَاهْدِنِي وَارْزُقْنِي».

Allaahummaghfir lee, warhamnee, wahdinee warzuqnee.

O Allāh forgive me, and have mercy on me, and guide me, and provide for me.[1]

263. Whenever anyone accepted Islam,

---

[1] Muslim 4/2072, Abu Dawud reports the same *Hadith* with the addition: and when the Arab left, the Prophet ﷺ said: "He has filled his hands with goodness." 1/220.

the Prophet ﷺ used to teach him how to pray, then he would instruct him to invoke Allāh with the following words:

«اللَّهُمَّ اغْفِرْ لِي، وَارْحَمْنِي، وَاهْدِنِي، وَعَافِنِي وَارْزُقْنِي».

Allaahummaghfir lee, warhamnee, wahdinee, wa 'aafinee warzuqnee.

O Allāh forgive me, and have mercy on me, and guide me, and give me good health and provide for me.[1]

264. The most excellent invocation is:

«الْحَمْدُ لِلَّهِ».

Alhamdu lillaah.

Praise is for Allāh,

and the most excellent words of remembrance are:

---

[1] Muslim 4/2073, and in one of Muslim's reports there is the addition: 'For these words combine [the goodness of] this world and the next.'

«لَا إِلَهَ إِلَّا اللهُ».

Laa 'ilaaha 'illallaah.

There is none worthy of worship but
Allāh.[1]

265. The good deeds which endure are:

«سُبْحَانَ اللهِ».

Subhaanallaah.

Glorified is Allāh, and

«وَالْحَمْدُ للهِ».

Walhamdu lillaah.

The praise is for Allāh, and

«وَلَا إِلَهَ إِلَّا اللهُ».

Wa laa 'ilaaha 'illallaah.

There is none worthy of worship but
Allāh, and

---

[1] At-Tirmiṭhi 5/462, Ibn Mājah 2/1249, and
Al-Hākim who graded it authentic and Aṯh-
Ṯhababi agreed 1/503. See Al-Albani, *Sahihul-
Jāmi' As-Saghir* 1/362.

«وَاللَّهُ أَكْبَرُ».

Wallaahu 'Akbar.

Allāh is the Most Great, and

«وَلَا حَوْلَ وَلَا قُوَّةَ إِلَّا بِاللَّهِ»

Wa laa hawla wa laa quwwata 'illaa billaah.

There is no power and no might except by Allāh.[1]

131. How the Prophet ﷺ glorified Allāh

266. Abdullah bin 'Amr ﷺ said: "I saw the Prophet ﷺ counting the glorification of his Lord on his right hand."[2]

---

[1] Ahmad (no. 513) (Ahmad Shakir, ed.) and its chain of narration is authentic. See *Majma'uz-Zawā'id* 1/297. Ibn Hajar mentions it in *Bulughul-Marām* saying that Ibn Hibbān and Al-Hākim considered it authentic.

[2] Abu Dawud with a different wording 2/81, and At-Tirmithi 5/521. See also Al-Albani, *Sahihul-Jāmi' As-Saghir* 4/271 (no. 4865).

132. Types of goodness and good etiquette for community life

267. When evening descends, bring your children indoors for the devils scatter out at this hour. Then after the passing of an hour (i.e. the first hour) of the night, (you may) let them (the children) go. Close your doors while mentioning the Name of Allāh, for the devil may not open a closed door. Fasten your waterskins mentioning the Name of Allāh. Cover your eating vessels mentioning the Name of Allāh even if you just put something over it, and extinguish your lamps.[1]

Peace and blessing be upon our Prophet, Muhammad, and upon his family and his Companions, all of them.

---

[1] Al-Bukhāri, cf. Al-Asqalāni, *Fathul-Bāri* 10/88, Muslim 3/1595.

TRANSLITERATION

In transliterating Arabic words the following system of symbols has been used:

Arabic script	English symbol	English words having similar sounds
أ	' ***	—
ب	b	bless
ت	t	true
ج	j	judge
ح	h**	—
خ	kh	—
د	d	dear
ذ	<u>th</u>	this
ر	r	road
ز	z	zoo
س	s	safe
ش	sh	show
ص	s**	—
ض	dh**	—
ط	t **	—

Arabic script	English symbol	English words having similar sounds
ظ	<u>dh</u>**	—
ع	' ***	—
غ	gh	—
ف	f	free
ق	q **	—
ك	k	kick
ل	l	light
م	m	moon
ن	n	nice
ه	h	health
و	w	wealth
ي	y	youth

* This symbol represents a glottal stop (transliterated medially and finally and not represented in transliteration when initial).

** These sounds have no equivalent sounds in English.

*** The Arabic sounds represented by the symbols (' / ') and the ones mentioned in the previous note are to be learned by imitating the native speakers of Arabic, if one wants to be exact in their pronunciation.

BIBLIOGRAPHY

Abu Dawud, *Sunan*

Ahmad bin Hanbal (d. 241 h.), *Al-Musnad*, 6 vols. Beirut: Al-Maktab Al-Islāmī.

Al-Albāni, Muhammad Nasir Ad-Dīn.

– *'Ahkāmul-Janā'iz.*

— *'Irwā'ul-Ghalīl.*

— *Mukhtasar Shamā'il At-Tirmithī.*

— *Sahih Al-'Adab Al-Mufrad.*

— *Sahihul-Jamī' As-Saghīr.*

– *Sahihut-Targhīb wat-Tarhīb.*

— *Sahih Sunan Ibn Mājah.*

— *Sahih Sunan At-Tirmithī.*

— *Silsilatul-'Ahādīth As-Sahīhah.*

Asqalāni Al-, see Ibn Hajar.

Baghawi, Abū Muhammad Al-Husain bin Mas'ūd Al-Farrā', Al-, (d. 516), *Ma'alam At-Tanzīl* (*Tafsīr Al-Baghawi*), in the margins of *Tafsīr Al-Khāzin*, 4 vols. Beirut: Dār Al-Fikr, 1979.

Bayhaqi, Abu Bakr Ahmad bin Husain bin 'Alī, Al-, (d. 458 h.),

— *As-Sunan Al-Kubra*, 10 vols. Beirut: Dār Al-Fikr, n.d.

— *Shu'ab Al-Imān.*

Bukhāri, Abī 'Abdullāh Muhammad bin Ismā'il bin Ibrāhīm bin Al-Mughīrah bin Bardizbah Al-Bukhāri Al-Ju'fī, Al-, (d. 256 h.),